THE

ENGLISH

LIBRARY

General Editor JAMES SUTHERLAND

Emeritus Professor of Modern Literature
University College, London

POETRY OF THE LANDSCAPE AND THE NIGHT

Two Eighteenth-century Traditions

Edited by
CHARLES PEAKE

Reader in English,
Queen Mary College, London

UNIVERSITY OF SOUTH CAROLINA PRESS

Columbia, S.C.

Published 1967 in Great Britain by
EDWARD ARNOLD (PUBLISHERS) LTD.
41 Maddox Street, London W.1

Published 1970 in the United States of America by the
UNIVERSITY OF SOUTH CAROLINA PRESS
Columbia, S.C. 29208

Standard Book Number: 87249–161–7
Library of Congress Catalog Card Number: 79–116474

Manufactured in Great Britain

General Preface

THE design of this series is to present fully annotated selections from English literature which will, it is hoped, prove satisfactory both in their breadth and their depth. To achieve this, some of the volumes have been planned so as to provide a varied selection from the poetry or prose of a limited period, which is both long enough to have developed a literary movement, and short enough to allow for adequate representation of the chief writers and of the various cross-currents within the movement. Examples of such periods are the late seventeenth century and the early eighteenth century. In other volumes the principle of selection is to present a literary kind (e.g. satirical poetry, the literary ballad). Here it is possible to cover a longer period without sacrificing the unified and comprehensive treatment which is the governing idea for the whole series. Other volumes, again, are designed to present a group of writers who form some kind of "school" (e.g. the Elizabethan sonneteers, the followers of Ben Jonson), or who were closely enough linked for their work to be brought together (e.g. the poetry of Johnson and Goldsmith).

Each volume has a full critical introduction. Headnotes, a special feature of this series, provide relevant background and critical comment for the individual poems and prose pieces. The footnotes are for the most part explanatory, giving as briefly as possible information about persons, places, allusions of one kind or another, the meaning of words, etc., which the twentieth-century reader is likely to require. Each selection aims at providing examples of the best work of the authors represented, but it is hoped that the inclusion of some less familiar pieces not available in any other collection will widen the reader's experience and enjoyment of the literature under review. The series is intended for use in universities and the upper forms of schools.

In this selection Mr. Peake has illustrated two of the most important kinds of poetry written in the eighteenth century: (1) the landscape (or "prospect") poem, descriptive often of some particular scene, and (2) the nocturnal poem, in which a dark night stirs "intimations of mortality and a consciousness of melancholy isolation", or a starry sky leads to "thoughts of the inconceivable vastness of the universe and the insignificance of mankind's place in it". The two genres are distinct, but they come together on the common ground of emotional meditation. Beginning with the seventeenth-century prototype *Cooper's Hill* (once a famous poem, and now hard to come by), the editor gives his readers a series of later landscape poems by such poets as Pope, Dyer, Thomson, and Cowper, culminating in Wordsworth's "Tintern Abbey"; and a parallel series of nocturnal poems (sometimes, but by no means always, involving meditation in a churchyard) from Lady Winchilsea's "Nocturnal Reverie" in the early part of the century to Coleridge's "Frost at Midnight" in 1798. Without unduly stretching his terms of reference the editor has been able to include in this volume much of the finest poetry written in the eighteenth century, and he has also found room for some attractive pieces by lesser-known poets. His selection should lead to a fuller understanding of the nature and range of eighteenth-century poetry.

Contents

Introduction

A PANORAMIC landscape can coax from the least philosophical mind speculations about the life which occupies the busy diminished creatures below,[1] or about the origins and forces of the natural world stretched out in perspective; and no great sensitiveness is required for a dark night to stir intimations of mortality and a consciousness of melancholy isolation, or for a starry sky to provoke thoughts of the inconceivable vastness of the universe and the insignificance of mankind's place in it. Like other men, poets easily become meditative when detached from their accustomed concerns and surroundings by space or darkness—although their meditations are more profound, imaginative and articulate—and poems involving distant prospects and the night can be found in the literature of many ages.

Yet during the eighteenth century such poems became particularly common, forming, in fact, two important and recognisable genres, each with its characteristic furniture. Landscapes regularly receded from a foreground cottage with smoking chimney to a middle distance of meadows, streams, woods and spires, set against a background of crags, crumbling towers and highlands, or culminated in a view of some friendly nobleman's country-home; while the night was full of owls, ravens, ruins, yew-trees and gravestones. Bad or mediocre writers pompously itemised such paraphernalia in conventional exercises, but similar materials were used variously and evocatively in the best work of such minor poets as Parnell and Dyer as well as in some of the finest poems of our literature. Many poets were content with a skilful blend of traditional ingredients, adding their own characteristic modifications and flavours, while others did not so much work in the genres as make use of them for quite new purposes; and, although not all eighteenth-century nature-poetry concerns landscapes and night-scenes, to follow the changes in the handling of these subjects is to trace some of the central elements in the poetry of the century.

There can be no adequate explanation of this (or any other) development in taste—too many things are involved—but there are some factors of obvious relevance. In the late seventeenth century, memories of the Civil War and subsequent uncertainties encouraged a dream of escape from the dangerous involvements of power, and many poets and essayists praised the

[1] Cf. Pope's remark quoted on p. 41.

charms of rural retirement. Sometimes they celebrated a Stoic withdrawal from the corruptions of the court and city, sometimes an Epicurean withdrawal to the comfortable and carefree delights of life on one's country estate, sometimes a Christian or neo-Platonic withdrawal to examine one's soul and commune with one's Maker—but, whatever the reason offered, a return to Nature was frequently advocated, in language and literary forms particularly indebted to Horace and Virgil,[1] as the way to true peace of mind. In the eighteenth century Virgil gradually became the dominant classical influence, and the emphasis fell on the need to understand and respond to the wonders of the natural universe, to perceive through them God's purpose and benevolence, and to acquire moral insights and stimuli to virtue. Much of this became merely fashionable, and rural retirement was praised by urban and sophisticated writers who would have been very unwilling for the countryside to occupy more than brief interludes in their lives. There were other aesthetic fashions at work which supported the literary one. For instance, at the beginning of the seventeenth century, one connoisseur remarked that landscape painting was so new to the English that they had to borrow a name for it (*landschap*) from the Dutch, but by the end of the century Claud Lorrain and Salvator Rosa had popularised new concepts of the beauty of extensive views. Similarly, in the eighteenth century, the enthusiasm for the expenditure of newly-acquired wealth on fine country-houses, landscape-gardening and topographical paintings influenced and was influenced by nature-poetry, and, more importantly, was a product of the same social and intellectual changes.

New discoveries in science (particularly Newton's discoveries in optics and cosmology) fostered the interest in natural phenomena; and religious thinkers, partly in response to the new science, considered God primarily as the omnipotent Creator whose nature might be apprehended through contemplation of his Creation. Increased urbanisation and the increased centralisation of wealth and power in a few big cities encouraged a nostalgia for country quiet, and improved communications made it easier to spend part of the year in London and part on one's country estate. Rising national pride required that England and her countryside should be honoured in verse as the Italian scene had been honoured by Virgil and other Latin poets, and the spread of literacy, which gradually freed writers from dependence on patronage, elevated the status of the poet, as a man of peculiar sensitivity whose emotional and instinctive reactions to natural beauty were in themselves of value. The Agrarian Revolution must also

[1] This is fully discussed in *The Happy Man: Studies in the Metamorphosis of a Classical Ideal, 1600–1700*, by Maren-Sofie Røstvig (Oxford: Blackwell, 1954).

have helped to focus interest on the rural scene; humanitarianism, especially towards the end of the century, drew attention to the conditions of the agricultural labouring-classes; and such religious movements as Evangelicism and Methodism also, through their stress on personal salvation, made lonely religious communion with Nature appear a source of spiritual help.

But it is one thing to point to a number of factors which in various ways influenced and shaped literary taste, and another to suppose that they constitute an adequate explanation of it. Similarly, although the influence of Virgil's *Georgics* is easily recognisable and almost pervasive, it is not possible to make an inclusive list of all the authors on whom the poets of the prospect and the night drew. The mark of one English poet is, however, as unmistakable and almost as widespread as Virgil's. Milton's "*L'Allegro*" and "*Il Penseroso*" provided much of the furniture I have already mentioned, and their spirit, diction, imagery, and, sometimes, versification can be detected in many of the poems of the two genres.

The prospect described in "*L'Allegro*" seems to be in England, but the scene is so beautifully idealised and wrapped in a golden classical haze that one is not surprised to find it inhabited by figures with Greek names:

> Streit mine eye hath caught new pleasures
> Whilst the Lantskip round it measures,
> Russet Lawns, and Fallows Gray
> Where the nibling flocks do stray,
> Mountains on whose barren brest
> The labouring clouds do often rest:
> Meadows trim with Daisies pide,
> Shallow Brooks, and Rivers wide.
> Towers, and Battlements it sees
> Boosom'd high in tufted Trees,
> Wher perhaps som beauty lies,
> The Cynosure of neighbouring eyes.
> Hard by, a Cottage chimney smokes,
> From betwixt two aged Okes,
> Where *Corydon* and *Thyrsis* met,
> Are at their savory dinner set
> Of Hearbs, and other Country Messes,
> Which the neat-handed *Phillis* dresses;
> And then in haste her Bowre she leaves,
> With *Thestylis* to bind the Sheaves.

In his evocation of the happy man, the harsher realities of peasant life were not to Milton's purpose. One advantage of the distant prospect was that it enabled the surveying eye to generalise and idealise, to adorn an English scene with pastoral charm akin to that draped by Theocritus and Virgil over their native lands, to ignore ugly or irrelevant detail, to see the strutting cock but not his midden.

Sir John Denham's *Cooper's Hill* (written later than Milton's two poems but published earlier) was equally important as a model for later poets,[1] though its mood and language were not so persistently influential. It is a poem which few now read, although Dryden declared that *Cooper's Hill* "for the majesty of the style is, and ever will be, the exact standard of good writing", and Dr. Johnson recognised it as the origin of "local poetry", the kind in which "the fundamental subject is some particular landscape, to be poetically described, with addition of such embellishments as may be supplied by historical retrospection or incidental meditation". Modern readers who complain of too little description and too much embellishment miss the point: Denham is not primarily concerned with the view but with an appeal to patriotism and political good sense. He conscientiously transplants the classical world to England: Cooper's Hill by Runnymede is his Parnassus and the Thames his Helicon, while to "a quick Poetick sight", he says, the river-valley is peopled not only with fairies but with satyrs, nymphs, and the courts of Faunus and Sylvanus. Old St. Paul's to the east and Windsor Castle to the west are the imagined limits of a scene which serves as an index to political lessons derivable from Nature and from history, and as a varied warning against disturbing the prospects of peace and wealth by factious discontent, destroying the ordained balance between King and people. Such an employment of landscape to introduce general observations concerning life and society became an important characteristic of the prospect tradition, though later writers tend to particularise more in describing the scene and to derive from it moral or spiritual rather than political insights and lessons.

Such developments are already evident in Pope's *Windsor-Forest*, despite the very marked indebtedness to Denham. Pope chooses the same scene, uses similar historical and mythical materials, makes hunting a central symbol, pays the same classical homage to his country's landscape, and has both a contemporary political reference and a vision of future power and prosperity. But although the forthcoming Treaty of Utrecht was the occasion for the completion and publication of the poem, it is in no sense its subject. Pope is dealing with a much more generalised concept of Peace. Denham refers to the charms of variety and to the blending of discordant elements in a universal harmony, but the notion of *discordia concors*, however

---

[1] Although a seventeenth-century poem, it is included in this volume because it is important in the landscape tradition and not easily available.

variously related to the scene, to the political situation, and to the order of creation, remains for the most part a concept understood rather than one which shapes the whole poem. Pope almost at once moves from a general image of the Forest to the harmonious confusion of Creation, and thence to a concept of "Order in Variety" which is at once a cosmological, social, political, international and aesthetic principle as well as a definition of the peace which he anticipates and welcomes; this principle controls the poem's whole emotional, intellectual, and imaginative character and progress. Similarly, although the landscape is, like Denham's, idealised, it is idealised more sensuously, and, at the same time, is more particularised and more thoroughly integrated into the total meaning of the poem.

Many of these differences are attributable to the fact that Denham was an accomplished poet and Pope a great one, but there are also signs in *Windsor-Forest* of those post-Restoration praises of rural retirement to which I have already referred. One can never be sure just how far a great poet is reflecting the spirit of his age and how far shaping it. But the nearly simultaneous appearance of Dyer's "Grongar Hill" and Thomson's *Winter* is strongly suggestive of a new taste for nature-poetry, where description, whether or not accompanied by general observations, does not depend on them for its justification. There had been many descriptive poems earlier in the century, besides such nocturnals as Lady Winchilsea's "Nocturnal Rêverie". Gay's *Rural Sports* and *Shepherd's Week* contained many vivid descriptive passages, as did such variations on the pastoral as Ambrose Philips's "Winter-Piece" and William Diaper's *Nereides: or Sea-Eclogues* and *Dryades*; and a whole group of so-called "physico-theological" poets had traced the hand of God in the created universe. But Dyer's and Thomson's poems seem to have something fresh: the natural scene seems more immediately present before the poet's and the reader's eyes, and (despite Thomson's frequent borrowings from Virgil) less dependent on classical colouring, overtones and allusions.

Critics have often perceived in "Grongar Hill" evidence of Dyer's skill as a painter, and, as often, more cautious critics have warned against such dangerous confusions of two distinct arts, and have pointed out that the poet's view is not only more extensive and various than could be accommodated on a canvas, but also changes as he climbs higher. Of course, verbal painting is only a metaphor, but there may, nevertheless, be something painterly about the way Dyer lays out his landscape and notes such details as "streaks of meadows" and distant steeples which, in the light of the setting sun, look like "ascending fires". At least, it can be said that Dyer has a special sensitiveness to form and colour, and that, compared to Thomson's moving and sometimes turbulent scenes, Dyer's are as motionless as painted landscapes. As for his moral reflections, they are so comfortably incorporated as humble truths worthy of remembrance that they do not disturb the sense of immediacy. Joseph Warton said perceptively of one of Dyer's moralising passages that it "imparts to us the same pleasure that we feel, when in wandering through a wilderness or grove, we suddenly behold in the turning of the walk, a statue of some VIRTUE or MUSE". The influence of Milton is apparent both in "Grongar Hill" and "A Country Walk", but Dyer's tone is more intimate and his view more familiar; instead of Corydon, a Wordsworthian old man puffs over his spade, while the cock, though modelled on the splendid bird in "L'Allegro", belongs more surely to the farmyard poultry.

The spirit of Dyer's pleasant and unforced variations on the prospect poem can be traced in numerous unpretentious verses evoking a scene or a time of day, but a much more powerful influence on the course of eighteenth-century poetry was exerted by The Seasons. Thomson, for all his manifold indebtedness, transformed the poetic presentation of external nature. He believed that it was in itself a theme and subject sufficient for a long and complex poem, and, although obviously no treatment of it could be exhaustive, he attempted to present all the main aspects and phenomena of nature, experienced and, as far as possible, explained. To this end he borrowed freely from earlier literary forms—georgics, eclogues, prospect and nocturnal poetry, hymns to the Creator—and as freely from science, geography, philosophy, theology, and any other branch of learning which came his way and was relevant to his purpose. Although he was ready to find in natural phenomena texts for patriotic addresses, moral lessons, scientific popularisations or celebrations of the divine benevolence, his descriptions do not depend on such justifications, and, at times, he seems to have Wordsworthian intuitions of a moral and spiritual power in Nature which might influence directly those who exposed themselves to it:

> I solitary court
> The inspiring Breeze and meditate the Book
> Of Nature, ever open, aiming thence
> Warm from the Heart to learn the moral Song.

Descriptive poetry was often said to lack action or moral truth, and is still belittled as mere verbal photography. But no poetic description can be that. What the poet's eye is drawn to, the way in which his imagination reacts, his manner of organising and synthesising the elements of his experience, the words in which he embodies it—all depend on his total poetic personality, his entire attitude to and view of life. Thomson found in the natural world a kind of vocabulary through which he could express his deepest intuitions more truthfully and exactly than in the language of philosophical or moralistic statement; his descriptions are as much part of his "meaning" as are the meditative, homiletic, theological or cosmological passages. Certainly "photographic" would be a thoroughly inept word for poetry which characteristically presents man confronted with the uncontrollable forces of the world he lives in—winds, torrents, storms, sunshine, growth. Thomson's prospects are rarely still: they move beneath a moving eye which can sweep over great expanses, rise above mountains, track the course of rivers, come close to observe how "from the bladed Field the fearful Hare / Limps awkward", or closer to note the brisk movements of the robin on "his slender Feet", or closer still to discern the microscopic creatures in the scum on ponds. For Thomson, "Full Nature swarms with Life"; he sees man, not against a beautiful but inanimate background, but as part of a living universe.

He is far loftier as well as more energetic and complex than Dyer, more reminiscent of *Paradise Lost* than of *"L'Allegro"*. Milton had set out to emulate the diction of the *Aeneid*; Thomson sets out, with Milton's help, to emulate that of the *Georgics*. The whole conception of *The Seasons* was that Nature was a subject worthy of the most elevated treatment and a style of high dignity, and, although there are pastoral-romantic, ironic and humorous interludes, the poem dwells on and reflects the grandeur of Creation. But the Miltonic-Virgilian influence is not simply a matter of inverted syntax, rhetorical phrasing, and Latinate constructions and vocabulary: more importantly it can be seen in the careful, subtle and extended shaping of sound, rhythm and syntax, to form a verbal equivalent of what is being described—see, for instance, the account of sea-birds disturbed by an approaching storm:

> The Cormorant on high
> Wheels from the Deep, and screams along the Land.
> Loud shrieks the soaring Hern; and with wild Wing
> The circling Sea-Fowl cleave the flaky Clouds.

The notion that Thomson invented English nature-poetry is, of course, naïvely absurd, yet it is true that no one had written of nature at this length or with this range, and one can concur with Dr. Johnson's verdict that "as a writer he is entitled to one praise of the highest kind: his mode of thinking and of expressing his thoughts is original".

Thomson sought factual accuracy as well as precision of expression. *The Seasons* is full of references to current scientific information and theories, and when the poet found he had been misinformed in some particular, he took care to correct the error in the next edition of his much-revised poem.

In this particularity he was following Virgil's example as well as that of his English predecessor, John Philips, whose *Cyder* (1708) is concerned with the art of growing apples. Thomson's scientific interest and enthusiasm were part of his whole apprehension of the natural world, and, thus, his information (even when mistaken) could be integrated into his poem. Something of the same spirit is found in such poems as Richard Savage's *The Wanderer* (1729), Dyer's *The Fleece* (1757), and Erasmus Darwin's *The Loves of the Plants* (1789), but already by Darwin's time the increasing specialisation of science was requiring new technical vocabularies and new modes of thought, unamenable to poetry. Though later poets have used scientific imagery, poetry has no longer seemed a proper vehicle for scientific instruction.

But there were other ways of handling the landscape in poetry. The sense of familiarity with a well-loved scene which characterises "Grongar Hill" was given a very different turn by the profoundly reflective and melancholic temperament of Thomas Gray. When Gray looked across the meadows towards Eton College (curiously, almost the same scene which had inspired Pope and Denham) he was not moved to classical reminiscence, historical celebration or patriotic fervour, but stirred by memories of past happiness known there—

> Where once my careless Childhood stray'd,
> A Stranger yet to Pain.

Gray's emotional and moral experience is much more subjective, introspective and searching than anything Dyer's quiet aphorisms could express. The scene and the boys occupying it become an image of human fate; the valley is transmuted into "the Vale of Years" in which all life's pains and terrors lie in wait for their victims; and Gray's own personal sense of loss is universalised into a perception of life as a bitter tragedy where to be a man is to be wretched. The poet's complete involvement in what lies before him rapidly blots out the historic or aesthetic qualities which Pope and Denham descried, as though the true subject of the poem is not what the poet has found in the scene but what the scene has found in him.

Poets have continued to find social, economic, political and aesthetic significances in landscape (Auden's "Dover 1937" is a fairly recent example), and the poet's intense emotional involvement with the scene before him is as evident in Wordsworth's "Tintern Abbey" or Dylan Thomas's "Over Sir John's hill" as in the Eton College ode. In the late eighteenth century both kinds of prospect were so common that Dr. Johnson declined to enumerate the "smaller poets, that have left scarce a corner of the island not dignified either by rhyme, or blank verse." But in the work of such major poets as Cowper and Wordsworth something of Thomson's descriptive energy and eye for detail was combined with the recognition of an emotional bond between the poet and his subject. The life of the poetic tradition which stemmed from Milton and Denham was sustained, not by conventional repetitions, but by those who brought to it new qualities and insights—who modified, adapted, and re-charged it with their own poetic vitality.

The same is true of the nocturnal tradition. Echoes of "*Il Penseroso*" long persisted, and Philomel, Cynthia, the curfew, the midnight hour, cloisters, the abbey's high-arched roof, the "dimm religious Light", the organ and choir, and "the peacefull Hermitage" all became familiar elements. But for the true poets these were like a musical theme on which to compose variations, or like familiar ground from which to base ventures into less-explored territories. Lady Winchilsea has her Philomel and "ancient Fabrick", but brings a peculiar sensitivity to the experience of falling dark-ness, and, although Parnell's "Night-Piece" is much closer to "*Il Penseroso*", it, too, has a manner quite its own, with its quiet argument spreading from the blue taper (which foreshadows thoughts of death) and culminating in Death's reproach to mankind and the vision of the soul soaring heaven-wards. Parnell would not have thought of the champing horse, and, if he had, would probably have seen no place for it in a serious poem, but, equally, Lady Winchilsea could not have managed the crisp, economical diction and the lucid process of the "Night-Piece".

To poets like these, a tradition was not a strait-jacket but a stimulus to which their natures and talents might respond: writers who are paralysed by conventions rarely have much poetic force to be inhibited. But while some poets achieved a personal idiom within a traditional scheme, others used the tradition for quite different ends. Gay, for instance, in the third section of *Trivia* is clearly not concerned with producing an ordinary nocturnal, any more than with writing an ordinary georgic, but he is able to use some familiar allusions and associations for humour or witty effect or to vary his poem with passages of serious and even gloomy reflection. Thomson, as I have already said, borrows just so much as he can shape into his larger view of man in relationship to God and the natural world. Even lesser figures, like Blair and Young, for all their echoes and conventional postures, brought new qualities to the nocturnal. *Night-Thoughts* intensified the melancholy meditations by pretending that the contest between despondency and faith was motivated by the poet's personal wretchedness, while *The Grave* drove home its morality with a grim insistence on the horrors of physical corruption. Neither poet was a profound thinker, and both, despite ecstasies about resurrection, seem to relish and cultivate a morbid gloom; but their immense popularity was not entirely due to a public appetite for emotionally-charged religious attitudinisings: their contemporaries (and readers for another hundred years) recognised the characteristic, if exaggerated, energy of their blank verse, and praised the novelty which the poets somewhat laboriously aimed at and spasmodically attained.

Both were more deliberately "original" than William Collins, although the "Ode to Evening" has demonstrated its originality on the minds of generations of readers. However derivative it may be in mood, content, imagery and diction, it registers as a distinct and wholly realised entity. Yet the nature of its uniqueness is very difficult to define. Modern criticism, which has excelled in the analysis of metaphysical wit, complex patterns of imagery and symbols, multiple levels of meaning, and the interplay between colloquial and poetic diction and rhythms, finds very little to get hold of in Collins's poem. Its quality can be more easily recognised than explained, although the sound of the poem—its movement and rhythms, the interplay of syntax and metre, the shifting pauses and stresses, the phrasing, the delicate placing of vowels and consonants—clearly plays an important part in the total effect. Satisfactory analysis of the function of sound in poetry may be impossible, but that is no reason for ignoring its importance: certainly much of the best poetry of the eighteenth century is directed as much to the ear as to the eye of the reader's imagination.

This applies not only to Thomson, Collins, and Cowper, but also to such minor poets as Thomas Warton and John Cunningham, who are often concerned primarily with the evocation of an experience where a human mood fuses with some aspect of the natural world. Gray's *Elegy* adds to such evocation a profound general meditation. As in the Eton College ode, the poet's personal feelings are related to universal truths, but whereas the ode spreads outwards from the memories of childhood to the generalisation about man's fate, the *Elegy* starts from the poet alone in the darkening churchyard, swells into the great monody on death, and then returns to connect the poet's own preoccupations with the wider vision of the un-honoured dead. The thought of the poem consists of this process, not of detachable aphorisms. Tennyson said that Gray's "divine platitudes" made him weep, but there are no platitudes in the poem, although some lines can be converted into platitudes by plucking them out of the magnificently integrated context of thought, emotion and imagination, fixed in words and verbal movements and sounds which seem to enact the whole process. Few would disagree with Dr. Johnson's judgment that "Had Gray written often thus it had been vain to blame, and useless to praise him."

In tracing both the nocturnal and the prospect traditions to Gray, I do not want to suggest that they culminated in his work and thereafter slowly expired. No worth-while tradition expires: its course is one of renewings, reshapings, and new applications, until the original forms have been so changed that they no longer exert a direct influence, and it becomes easier to talk in terms of a new tradition. *The Seasons* was already a long way from the landscape and night poems which preceded it and on which it drew, and its impact was such that later poets more frequently followed Thomson than Milton, Denham, or his other predecessors. It is certainly Thomson whose influence is most recognisable in Cowper's *The Task*, a poem which makes an equally free use of the genres but goes even farther from their spirit. When Cowper climbs a hill much of his pleasure is in his recognition of what he has often seen and long loved; when evening approaches his house, it is not as a spectre or a grey-sandalled nymph, but as a buxom matron with a tea-tray. Thomson was stirred by the mighty and sublime aspects of Nature: Cowper is more interested in the daily round than in the grand or extraordinary. Probably this difference is partly in the nature of the two men; Thomson seems to have been a plump and contented man who could afford temperamentally to enjoy the alarming and awe-inspiring, while Cowper, tormented by fears of the recurring madness in which he believed himself to be singled out among men for eternal damnation, comforted himself with tame hares, newspapers, quiet friendships, and surroundings in which he could feel peacefully at home. On the only occasion after he had settled at Olney that he was persuaded to leave it, he was uneasy:

> The cultivated appearance of Weston [near Olney] suits my frame of mind far better than wild hills that aspire to be mountains, covered with vast unfrequented woods, and here and there affording a peep between their summits at the distant ocean. Within doors all was hospitality and kindness, but the scenery *would* have its effect; and though delightful in the extreme to those who had spirits to bear it, was too gloomy for me.

This overpowering scenery was not that of the Scottish Highlands or the Lake District, but that of the South Downs near Chichester.

A poet who brought such painfully sensitive nerves to the contemplation of Nature was bound to react acutely but perhaps idiosyncratically. Though, like others, he might be moved by the picturesque isolation of a cottage on a hilltop, his enthusiasm for it quickly diminished when he found it lacked a water-supply—

> If solitude make scant the means of life,
> Society for me!

There is a change, too, in the ordering of poems. While Thomson (though not to Dr. Johnson's satisfaction) had tried to follow a coherent and methodical sequence in each part of *The Seasons*, Cowper's *The Task* is deliberately casual and digressive, started as a form of psychotherapy and following a course determined by intuition or random thoughts. Partly this is attributable to Cowper's special circumstances and partly to a conscious reaction against the planned and rationally-ordered literature of the earlier part of the century—a reaction also evident in such works as Churchill's *Gotham* and Sterne's *Tristram Shandy*—but it is also partly a consequence of the growing interest in the figure of the Poet, as an exceptional man, the processes of whose mind are almost as interesting as its products. At its worst this led to the chatty ramblings of long-winded versifiers, but at its best it led to the conversational ease of "Frost at Midnight", which, for all its hesitations and shifts of thought, does not wander, but represents the wanderings of the mind. It led also to *The Prelude; or, Growth of a Poet's Mind*, where Wordsworth was able to order his vision of man and the universe in direct relation to the nature and development of his own experiences. But although *The Prelude* has night-pieces and prospects, and historical links with the genres can be demonstrated, the demonstration would seem irrelevant: the essential qualities are now far removed from *Cooper's Hill* or "*Il Penseroso*". Even in "Tintern Abbey", which proceeds in familiar fashion from the landscape to personal associations and thence to the universal spirit which "rolls through all things", despite obvious connections with the Eton College ode and certain poems of nostalgic recollection, one is more aware of differences from than resemblances to the original forms of "local poetry".

Similarly it would be truer to say that "Tam o' Shanter" springs from the nocturnal tradition than that it is part of it. I know of no other poem, let alone one of comparable distinction and spirit, which first appeared as a footnote in a work of antiquarian scholarship, but the same human interest in ruins and death which showed in poems like Parnell's "Night-Piece" was one of the forces behind the enthusiastic antiquarianism in which so many of the poets were involved. Burns has his owlets and his dimly-lit ruins, but native (even local) witches dance in a ring in Alloway Kirk instead of the circling nymphs whose nightly dance was fearfully spied on in Diaper's *Dryades* (1712) and referred to in Joseph Warton's "Evening". Burns brings comic earthiness to a long-established series of churchyard encounters between mortals and spirits, and the sombre tradition serves mainly as a dark background to set off his glowing humour.

All of these changes can, in one way or another, be related to a kind of realism (oddly present in the so-called romanticism of the late eighteenth century) which can be seen in Cowper's treatment of daily life, the psychological realism of "Frost at Midnight", Wordsworth's use in poetry of "a selection of the real language of men", Burns's down-to-earth humour, and Crabbe's presentation of the sordid and unpleasant side of rural life. But these are not reflections of a change from stifling literary conventions to simple truth. They are rather signs of the emergence of a new set of conventions and traditions better suited to the kind of things poets at the end of the century wished to express. The earlier poets were as deeply concerned with human nature and experience, with man and his environment, but in different ways: for instance, although Parnell's diction is less colloquial than that of James Hurdis, and his conduct of a poem more disciplined by an awareness of literary tradition, he nevertheless speaks more directly of the human condition. In so far as this collection has a central purpose, it is to show not how the "Romantics" broke the chains of tradition, but how their works were part of a continuous process of change which lasted throughout the eighteenth century (and began before it and continued after it), of which some manifestations can be traced and examined in poems which in varying ways found their starting-point in man's experience of landscape and of night.

In this volume it has been impossible to adhere to the general policy of the series of including only whole poems or sections of poems. Thomson, Cowper, Young, Blair and Crabbe were too important to be omitted, but could not be represented by entire poems for reasons of space, and a few minor figures have also been represented by samples. I have, however, chosen passages of sufficient length and integrity to be representative. The other intention of the series, to put before students reliable first-edition texts, I have varied from in only three instances—*Cooper's Hill*, *The Seasons*, and "Grongar Hill"—where there were special reasons for using later editions. Eighteenth-century poets generally used rhetorical rather than logical punctuation, and the exertions of some editors to systematize punctuation have often reduced fluent verse to a crippled hopping from comma to comma. In some respects printing practice has changed, but the modern reader is rarely left in any real doubt, and I have tampered with the first editions only to the extent of removing insignificant italics (i.e. when they do not indicate a stress or emphasis, or mark an antithesis or personification), correcting a few obvious misprints, and introducing the modern conventions for the use of the possessive apostrophe. In a few other places punctation has been added or changed, but all these latter emendations are indicated in the introductory notes. Thus those who find no obstacles to their enjoyment and understanding of the poems as printed here can be certain that they will find little difficulty in reading eighteenth-century poetry in eighteenth-century editions.

Sir John Denham

COOPER'S HILL

Cooper's Hill is now more often referred to than read, but in the early eighteenth century it was considered one of the great poems of our literature, and Denham was regarded as sharing with Waller and Dryden the claim to have re-created English poetry and versification. The famous lines comparing the poetic ideal to the Thames (ll. 189–92) were so frequently echoed and imitated that in "Apollo's Edict" (1728), a poem usually attributed to Jonathan Swift, the god warned poets against the practice:

> For know I cannot bear to hear,
> The Mimickry of *deep yet clear*.

But as other poems in this collection show, the warning was not heeded.

Swift's allegorisation of Denham in *The Battle of the Books* (1704), as "a stout Modern, who from his father's side derived his lineage from Apollo, but his mother was of mortal race", recognises the prosaic streak in Denham's verse. Those who approach *Cooper's Hill* expecting natural description like that in the tradition of landscape poetry which developed from Denham's poem are likely to be disappointed. In many ways the poem has less to do with "Tintern Abbey" than with the patriotic sonnets Wordsworth wrote when fearing a French invasion. It was written in response to the political and religious unrest which broke out in civil war in the year the poem was published, and it aimed at pleasing persuasion rather than poetic transport. The satisfactions it has to offer are those of a skilfully conducted argument, enriched with appropriate imagery, economical and stately diction, and illustrative episodes. The stag-hunt is not difficult to enjoy, but full appreciation of the poem demands a grasp of its total conduct, and of the varied ways Denham uses the features of the landscape to celebrate Charles I as soldier and saint, to denounce religious fanaticism, and to advocate a proper balance of rights and duties between king and people.

The first edition of 1642 was unauthorised and incomplete, and the text given here is from the last version to appear during Denham's life-time, in *Poems and Translations* (1668): this was the version familiar to the eighteenth century. I have varied from it only where necessary—i.e. full-stops have been inserted at the ends of lines 212 and 232, and quotation marks

at the end of line 342; full-stops have been replaced by commas at the ends
of lines 39 and 200; and the comma in line 90 has been placed after "know"
instead of after "well".

> Sure there are Poets which did never dream
> Upon Parnassus, nor did tast the stream
> Of Helicon, we therefore may suppose
> Those made not Poets, but the Poets those.
> 5 And as Courts make not Kings, but Kings the Court,
> So where the Muses & their train resort,
> Parnassus stands; if I can be to thee
> A Poet, thou Parnassus art to me.
> Nor wonder, if (advantag'd in my flight,
> 10 By taking wing from thy auspicious height)
> Through untrac't ways, and aery paths I fly,
> More boundless in my Fancy than my eie:
> My eye, which swift as thought contracts the space
> That lies between, and first salutes the place
> 15 Crown'd with that sacred pile, so vast, so high,
> That whether 'tis a part of Earth, or sky,
> Uncertain seems, and may be thought a proud
> Aspiring mountain, or descending cloud,
> Paul's, the late theme of such a Muse whose flight
> 20 Has bravely reach't and soar'd above thy height:
> Now shalt thou stand though sword, or time, or fire,

Title: Cooper's Hill is on the south bank of the Thames facing Runny-
mede.

2 *Parnassus:* a twin-peaked mountain in Greece, sacred to Apollo, God
of Poetry, and to the Muses.

3 *Helicon:* a mountain in Greece, whence sprang the Muses' fountains,
symbolic of inspiration.

6 *train:* followers.

11 *untrac't:* untrodden. Denham was aware that he was attempting
something new.

15 *pile:* any large building.

19-20 *(Marginal note, 1668:* "M.W.") i.e. Mr. Waller. Edmund Waller
had celebrated Charles I's renovation of St. Paul's, in the 1630s, with a
poem, "Upon His Majesty's Repairing of St. Paul's". The reference is, of
course, to *Old* St. Paul's.

Or zeal more fierce than they, thy fall conspire,
Secure, whilst thee the best of Poets sings,
Preserv'd from ruine by the best of Kings.
25   Under his proud survey the City lies,
And like a mist beneath a hill doth rise;
Whose state and wealth the business and the crowd,
Seems at this distance but a darker cloud:
And is to him who rightly things esteems,
30   No other in effect than what it seems:
Where, with like hast, though several ways, they run
Some to undo, and some to be undone;
While luxury, and wealth, like war and peace,
Are each the other's ruine, and increase;
35   As Rivers lost in Seas some secret vein
Thence reconveighs, there to be lost again.
Oh happiness of sweet retir'd content!
To be at once secure, and innocent.
Windsor the next (where Mars with Venus dwells,
40   Beauty with strength) above the Valley swells
Into my eye, and doth it self present
With such an easie and unforc't ascent,
That no stupendious precipice denies
Access, no horror turns away our eyes:

22 *zeal:* religious fanaticism.

27 *state:* costly display. (The comparison with wealth is repeated in ll. 33–4.)   *business:* busy activity.

30 *in effect:* in reality. (Denham's point is that the pursuit of wealth and luxury is like pursuing shadows in a fog.)

31 *several:* differing.   **32** *undo:* ruin.

35 *some secret vein:* It was a common belief that rivers were formed by sea-water sucked up through sandy strata of the earth, and re-emerging, purified, in highlands.

39 *where Mars with Venus dwells:* (*Marginal note, 1668:* "Windsor".) The Roman Gods of War and Love stand for Windsor's military strength and beauty, as well as for Charles I and his queen.

43 *stupendious:* dizzying.

44 *horror:* Applied to landscape, the word means "wild and repellent or awesome feature".

45 But such a Rise, as doth at once invite
 A pleasure, and a reverence from the sight.
 Thy mighty Master's Embleme, in whose face
 Sate meekness, heightned with Majestick Grace
 Such seems thy gentle height, made only proud
50 To be the basis of that pompous load,
 Than which, a nobler weight no Mountain bears,
 But Atlas only that supports the Sphears.
 When Nature's hand this ground did thus advance,
 'Twas guided by a wiser power than Chance;
55 Mark't out for such a use, as if 'twere meant
 T' invite the builder, and his choice prevent.
 Nor can we call it choice, when what we chuse,
 Folly, or blindness only could refuse.
 A Crown of such Majestick towrs doth Grace
60 The Gods' great Mother, when her heavenly race
 Do homage to her, yet she cannot boast
 Amongst that numerous, and Celestial host,
 More Heros than can Windsor, nor doth Fame's
 Immortal book record more noble names.
65 Not to look back so far, to whom this Isle
 Owes the first Glory of so brave a pile,
 Whether to Caesar, Albanact, or Brute,

47 *Master:* King Charles I. 50 *pompous:* magnificent.
52 *Atlas:* the North African mountain, identified with the giant, who, in classical myths upheld the sky.
53 *advance:* raise up.
56 *his choice prevent:* leave him with no choice but to build there.
60 *The Gods' great Mother:* Cybele, mother of the gods, was represented as wearing a turreted crown.
60 *race:* family.
67–70 Windsor Castle was built by William the Conqueror on the site of an earlier fortress. Denham is speculating about the original builders of this fortress: Julius Caesar, first Roman invader; Brut (or Brutus), descended from the Trojan Aeneas, and, according to legend, first king of Britain; his son, Albanact, who became first king of Scotland; King Arthur, the legendary ruler of the Britons; or Canute, the Danish king of England. Thus Romans, Trojans, Scots, Britons and Danes might all claim to have founded Windsor, as after Homer's death seven cities disputed the honour

The Brittish Arthur, or the Danish Knute,
(Though this of old no less contest did move,
70 Then when for Homer's birth seven Cities strove)
(Like him in birth, thou should'st be like in fame,
As thine his fate, if mine had been his Flame)
But whosoere it was, Nature design'd
First a brave place, and then as brave a mind.
75 Not to recount those several Kings, to whom
It gave a Cradle, or to whom a Tombe,
But thee (great Edward) and thy greater son,
(The lillies which his Father wore, he won)
And thy Bellona, who the Consort came
80 Not only to thy Bed, but to thy Fame,
She to thy Triumph led one Captive King,
And brought that son, which did the second bring.
Then didst thou found that Order (whither love

of having been his birthplace.   (*Contest* (l. 69) should be stressed on the
second syllable.)

72 *Flame:* inspiration or genius.   **74** *brave:* noble.

75 *Not to recount:* Parallel in construction to l. 65. (It is not necessary to
go back to the founders or name all the kings (except Edward III) to show
the superiority of Windsor's heroes to Cybele's.)

77-8 (*Marginal note, 1668:* "Edward the third, and the Black Prince".)
Edward III was born at Windsor; his son, the Black Prince, was neither
born nor buried there. *But:* except.

78 *lillies:* In 1340, Edward III claimed the French throne and included the
fleur-de-lis in his coat of arms. The victories of his son gave substance to
the claim.

79 *Bellona:* (*Marginal note, 1668:* "Queen Philip"). i.e. Queen Philippa,
wife of Edward III, buried at Windsor. Bellona was the Roman goddess
of war.

81-2 (*Marginal note, 1668:* "The Kings of France and Scotland".) Queen
Philippa was credited with the capture of David II of Scotland, and her
son, the Black Prince, captured John II of France at Poitiers. Both kings
were imprisoned at Windsor. *Triumph:* Victory procession.

83-4 Two reasons were commonly given for Edward III's founding of
the Order of the Garter: to commemorate the victories of Crecy and Calais,
or to cover the confusion of the Countess of Salisbury when she lost her
garter.   *whither:* whether.

Or victory thy Royal thoughts did move)
85 Each was a noble cause, and nothing less,
Than the design, has been the great success:
Which forraign Kings, and Emperors esteem
The second honour to their Diadem.
Had thy great Destiny but given thee skill,
90 To know, as well as power to act her will,
That from those Kings, who then thy captives were,
In after-times should spring a Royal pair
Who should possess all that thy mighty power,
Or thy desires more mighty, did devour;
95 To whom their better Fate reserves what ere
The Victor hopes for, or the Vanquisht fear;
That bloud, which thou and thy great Grandsire shed,
And all that since these sister Nations bled,
Had been unspilt, had happy Edward known
100 That all the bloud he spilt, had been his own.
When he that Patron chose, in whom are joyn'd
Souldier and Martyr, and his arms confin'd
Within the Azure Circle, he did seem
But to foretell, and prophesie of him,
105 Who to his Realms that Azure round hath joyn'd,
Which Nature for their bound at first design'd.
That bound, which to the World's extreamest ends,

92 *a Royal pair:* King Charles I and his wife, Henrietta Maria. Neither was directly descended from David II and John II, but they were descended from the Scottish and French royal houses respectively.

95–6 Charles and his Queen ruled over a rich and powerful England such as Edward III hoped for and the captive kings feared.

97 *Grandsire:* Edward I. (The reference is to his Scottish wars.)

99 *happy:* i.e. Edward III would have been happy (fortunate) if he had known.

101 *Patron:* St. George, the patron saint of the Order of the Garter, was reputedly a soldier who was martyred at Lydda in Palestine.

103 *Azure Circle:* The arms of the Order consist of the red cross of St. George surrounded by a blue garter.

104–5 The arms seem prophetic of a king (Charles I) who would be soldier and saint, and would rule the ocean. Denham could not have foreseen in 1642 that the king would also become known as "the Royal martyr".

Endless it self, its liquid arms extends;
Nor doth he need those Emblemes which we paint,
110 But is himself the Souldier and the Saint.
Here should my wonder dwell, & here my praise,
But my fixt thoughts my wandring eye betrays,
Viewing a neighbouring hill, whose top of late
A Chappel crown'd, till in the Common Fate,
115 The adjoyning Abby fell: (may no such storm
Fall on our times, where ruine must reform.)
Tell me (my Muse) what monstrous dire offence,
What crime could any Christian King incense
To such a rage? was't Luxury, or Lust?
120 Was he so temperate, so chast, so just?
Were these their crimes? they were his own much more:
But wealth is Crime enough to him that's poor,
Who having spent the Treasures of his Crown,
Condemns their Luxury to feed his own.
125 And yet this Act, to varnish o're the shame
Of sacriledge, must bear devotion's name.
No Crime so bold, but would be understood
A real, or at least a seeming good.
Who fears not to do ill, yet fears the Name,
130 And free from Conscience, is a slave to Fame.
Thus he the Church at once protects, & spoils:
But Princes' swords are sharper than their stiles.
And thus to th' ages past he makes amends,
Their Charity destroys, their Faith defends.

113 *neighbouring hill:* St. Anne's hill, Chertsey.

115 *Abby:* Chertsey Abbey.

116 *ruine must reform:* Denham fears that attempts to reform the Church will ruin it, as did the earlier Reformation.

117-9 a Virgilian allusion. (See *Aeneid* i, 8–11.) *King:* Henry VIII.

131-2 These lines allude to the title of *Fidei Defensor* given to Henry VIII for his book against Luther. Denham regards the king as a more effective destroyer with his sword than defender with his pen. "Stiles" is a pun, referring both to writing instruments (Latin, *stilus*) and to manner of writing.

134-6 The destruction of the abbeys ended the charitable work of the monks, leaving them only the contemplative life.

135 Then did Religion in a lazy Cell,
In empty, airy contemplations dwell;
And like the block, unmoved lay: but ours,
As much too active, like the stork devours.
Is there no temperate Region can be known,
140 Betwixt their Frigid, and our Torrid Zone?
Could we not wake from that Lethargick dream,
But to be restless in a worse extream?
And for that Lethargy was there no cure,
But to be cast into a Calenture?
145 Can knowledge have no bound, but must advance
So far, to make us wish for ignorance?
And rather in the dark to grope our way,
Than led by a false guide to erre by day?
Who sees these dismal heaps, but would demand
150 What barbarous Invader sackt the land?
But when he hears, no Goth, no Turk did bring
This desolation, but a Christian King;
When nothing, but the Name of Zeal, appears
'Twixt our best actions and the worst of theirs,
155 What does he think our Sacriledge would spare,
When such th' effects of our devotions are?
Parting from thence 'twixt anger, shame, & fear,
Those for whats past, & this for whats too near:
My eye descending from the Hill, surveys
160 Where Thames amongst the wanton vallies strays.
Thames, the most lov'd of all the Ocean's sons,
By his old Sire to his embraces runs,
Hasting to pay his tribute to the Sea,

137–8 In the fable the frogs complained of their dull King Log (or Block);
he was replaced by King Stork, who devoured the frogs. Similarly the inert
religious life of the monks has been replaced by fanatical and dangerous
puritanism.
   144 *Calenture:* feverish delirium and hallucinations.
   160 (*Marginal note, 1668:* "Thames"). *wanton:* (i) wandering unpredict-
ably, and (ii) luxuriant.
   161 *Ocean's sons:* All rivers were supposedly the children of Oceanus and
Tethys. (See ll. 35–6 and note.)

Like mortal life to meet Eternity.
165 Though with those streams he no resemblance hold,
     Whose foam is Amber, and their Gravel Gold;
     His genuine, and less guilty wealth t' explore,
     Search not his bottom, but survey his shore;
     Ore which he kindly spreads his spacious wing,
170 And hatches plenty for th' ensuing Spring.
     Nor then destroys it with too fond a stay,
     Like Mothers which their Infants overlay.
     Nor with a sudden and impetuous wave,
     Like profuse Kings, resumes the wealth he gave.
175 No unexpected inundations spoyl
     The mower's hopes, nor mock the plowman's toyl:
     But God-like his unwearied Bounty flows;
     First loves to do, then loves the Good he does.
     Nor are his Blessings to his banks confin'd,
180 But free, and common, as the Sea or Wind;
     When he to boast, or to disperse his stores
     Full of the tributes of his grateful shores,
     Visits the world, and in his flying towers
     Brings home to us, and makes both Indies ours;
185 Finds wealth where 'tis, bestows it where it wants
     Cities in deserts, woods in Cities plants.
     So that to us no thing, no place is strange,
     While his fair bosom is the world's exchange.
     O could I flow like thee, and make thy stream
190 My great example, as it is my theme!

165-6 The river Eridanus (now the Po) was, according to the Greeks, a source of amber. (It has been suggested that the reason for this legend was that Greek traders fetched amber from the mouth of the Po, whither it had been brought across Europe from the Baltic area.) The river Hermus and its tributary the Pactolus, in Asia Minor, were famous for the gold in their gravelly beds.

171 The Thames does not cause prolonged flooding.

172 *overlay:* suffocate by lying on them while asleep.

174 *resumes:* takes back.   **180** *common:* given to all.

183 *flying towers:* sailing ships.

188 *exchange:* market.

> Though deep, yet clear, though gentle, yet not dull,
> Strong without rage, without ore-flowing full.
> Heaven her Eridanus no more shall boast,
> Whose Fame in thine, like lesser Currents lost,
> 195 Thy Nobler streams shall visit Jove's aboads,
> To shine amongst the Stars, and bath the Gods.
> Here Nature, whether more intent to please
> Us or her self, with strange varieties,
> (For things of wonder give no less delight
> 200 To the wise Maker's, than beholders' sight,
> Though these delights from several causes move
> For so our children, thus our friends we love)
> Wisely she knew, the harmony of things,
> As well as that of sounds, from discords springs.
> 205 Such was the discord, which did first disperse
> Form, order, beauty through the Universe;
> While driness moysture, coldness heat resists,
> All that we have, and that we are, subsists.
> While the steep horrid roughness of the Wood
> 210 Strives with the gentle calmness of the flood.

193 *Eridanus:* See note on ll. 165–6. The name was also given to a winding constellation in the southern hemisphere.

196 *bath:* i.e. bathe.

197 (*Marginal note, 1668:* "The Forest".) The note merely marks the transition from the river Thames to Windsor Forest.

201 *several:* separate, distinct.

205–6 The creation of the universe was often compared to harmony. (Cf. Dryden's "From Harmony, from heav'nly Harmony / This universal Frame began": *A Song for St. Cecilia's Day.* See, too, *Windsor-Forest*, p. 43, ll. 13–14.) Denham's point is that before there can be harmony, the various discordant notes must be separated from each other. Similarly in Chaos all the elements were confused together, and had to be separated and opposed before they could be harmoniously related in the act of Creation. On their continued separateness the universe depends. The centrality of this concept of *discordia concors* in *Cooper's Hill* and *Windsor-Forest* is discussed at length by Earl R. Wasserman in *The Subtler Language* (O.U.P., 1959).

209 *horrid:* bristling, shaggy.

Such huge extreams when Nature doth unite,
Wonder from thence results, from thence delight.
The stream is so transparent, pure, and clear,
That had the self-enamour'd youth gaz'd here,
215 So fatally deceiv'd he had not been,
While he the bottom, not his face had seen.
But his proud head the aery Mountain hides
Among the Clouds; his shoulders, and his sides
A shady mantle cloaths; his curled brows
220 Frown on the gentle stream, which calmly flows,
While winds and storms his lofty forehead beat:
The common fate of all that's high or great.
Low at his foot a spacious plain is plac't,
Between the mountain and the stream embrac't:
225 Which shade and shelter from the Hill derives,
While the kind river wealth and beauty gives;
And in the mixture of all these appears
Variety, which all the rest indears.
This scene had some bold Greek, or Brittish Bard
230 Beheld of old, what stories had we heard,
Of Fairies, Satyrs, and the Nymphs their Dames,
Their feasts, their revels, & their amorous flames.
'Tis still the same, although their aery shape
All but a quick Poetick sight escape.
235 There Faunus and Sylvanus keep their Courts,
And thither all the horned hoast resorts,
To graze the ranker mead, that noble heard
On whose sublime and shady fronts is rear'd
Nature's great Master-piece; to shew how soon
240 Great things are made, but sooner are undone.

214 (*Marginal note, 1668:* "Narcissus".) Narcissus fell in love with his
own reflection.
219 In the personification of the mountain, trees become his cloak, and
the overhanging crags of the summit his brows.
235 *Faunus and Sylvanus:* the Roman gods of agriculture, and of fields
and forests respectively.
236 *horned hoast:* deer.   237 *ranker mead:* more luxuriant meadowland.
239–40 The deer's antlers are grown and shed each year.

Here have I seen the King, when great affairs
Give leave to slacken, and unbend his cares,
Attended to the Chase by all the flower
Of youth, whose hopes a Nobler prey devour:
245 Pleasure with Praise, & danger, they would buy,
And wish a foe that would not only fly.
The stagg now conscious of his fatal Growth,
At once indulgent to his fear and sloth,
To some dark covert his retreat had made,
250 Where nor man's eye, nor heaven's should invade
His soft repose; when th' unexpected sound
Of dogs, and men, his wakeful ear doth wound.
Rouz'd with the noise, he scarce believes his ear,
Willing to think th' illusions of his fear
255 Had given this false Alarm, but straight his view
Confirms, that more than all he fears is true.
Betray'd in all his strengths, the wood beset,
All instruments, all Arts of ruine met;
He calls to mind his strength, and then his speed,
260 His winged heels, and then his armed head;
With these t' avoid, with that his Fate to meet:
But fear prevails, and bids him trust his feet.
So fast he flyes, that his reviewing eye
Has lost the chasers, and his ear the cry;
265 Exulting, till he finds, their Nobler sense
Their disproportion'd speed does recompense.
Then curses his conspiring feet, whose scent
Betrays that safety which their swiftness lent.

---

241 *the King:* Charles I.

244 The young men hope for a chance of distinguishing themselves in battle.

258 *instruments:* may refer to all the huntsmen, horses, dogs, as well as to their weapons and equipment. (The "Arts" are the management and use of all these "instruments".)

263 *reviewing:* backward-looking.

265 *Nobler sense:* intelligence.

267 *conspiring:* secretly aiding his enemies.

Then tries his friends, among the baser herd,
270 Where he so lately was obey'd, and fear'd,
His safety seeks: the herd, unkindly wise,
Or chases him from thence, or from him flies.
Like a declining States-man, left forlorn
To his friends' pity, and pursuers' scorn,
275 With shame remembers, while himself was one
Of the same herd, himself the same had done.
Thence to the coverts, & the conscious Groves,
The scenes of his past triumphs, and his loves;
Sadly surveying where he rang'd alone
280 Prince of the soyl, and all the herd his own;
And like a bold Knight Errant did proclaim
Combat to all, and bore away the Dame;
And taught the woods to eccho to the stream
His dreadful challenge, and his clashing beam.
285 Yet faintly now declines the fatal strife;
So much his love was dearer than his life.
Now every leaf, and every moving breath
Presents a foe, and every foe a death.
Wearied, forsaken, and pursu'd, at last
290 All safety in despair of safety plac'd,
Courage he thence resumes, resolv'd to bear
All their assaults, since 'tis in vain to fear.
And now too late he wishes for the fight
That strength he wasted in Ignoble flight:
295 But when he sees the eager chase renew'd,
Himself by dogs, the dogs by men pursu'd:
He straight revokes his bold resolve, and more
Repents his courage, than his fear before;
Finds that uncertain waies unsafest are,
300 And Doubt a greater mischief than Despair.
Then to the stream, when neither friends, nor force,
Nor speed, nor Art avail, he shapes his course;

277 *conscious:* witnessing.
284 *beam:* the main branch of a stag's horns.
299 *uncertain waies:* changing policies.

Thinks not their rage so desperate t' assay
An Element more merciless than they.
305 But fearless they pursue, nor can the floud
Quench their dire thirst; alas, they thirst for bloud.
So towards a Ship the oarefin'd Gallies ply,
Which wanting Sea to ride, or wind to fly,
Stands but to fall reveng'd on those that dare
310 Tempt the last fury of extream despair.
So fares the Stagg among th' enraged Hounds,
Repels their force, and wounds returns for wounds.
And as a Hero, whom his baser foes
In troops surround, now these assails, now those,
315 Though prodigal of life, disdains to die
By common hands; but if he can descry
Some nobler foe's approach, to him he calls,
And begs his Fate, and then contented falls.
So when the King a mortal shaft lets fly
320 From his unerring hand, then glad to dy,
Proud of the wound, to it resigns his bloud,
And stains the Crystal with a Purple floud.
This a more Innocent, and happy chase,
Than when of old, but in the self-same place,
325 Fair liberty pursu'd, and meant a Prey
To lawless power, here turn'd, and stood at bay.
When in that remedy all hope was plac't
Which was, or should have been at least, the last.
Here was that Charter seal'd, wherein the Crown
330 All marks of Arbitrary power lays down:
Tyrant and slave, whose names of hate and fear,
The happier stile of King and Subject bear:

303 *assay:* venture in.
307 *oarefin'd:* equipped with oars like fins.
308 *wanting Sea to ride:* lacking enough water to float. (The ship would be waiting for a tide.)
324-6 (*Marginal note, 1668:* 'Runny Mead where that great Charter was first sealed".)
327 *that remedy:* i.e. rebellion.
329 *that Charter:* (*Marginal note, 1668:* "Magna Charta").

Happy, when both to the same Center move,
When Kings give liberty, and Subjects love.
335   Therefore not long in force this Charter stood;
Wanting that seal, it must be seal'd in bloud.
The Subjects arm'd, the more their Princes gave,
Th' advantage only took the more to crave.
Till Kings by giving, give themselves away,
340   And even that power, that should deny, betray.
"Who gives constrain'd, but his own fear reviles
"Not thank't, but scorn'd; nor are they gifts, but spoils."
Thus Kings, by grasping more than they could hold,
First made their Subjects by oppression bold:
345   And popular sway, by forcing Kings to give
More than was fit for Subjects to receive,
Ran to the same extreams; and one excess
Made both, by striving to be greater, less.
When a calm River rais'd with sudden rains,
350   Or Snows dissolv'd, oreflows th' adjoyning Plains,
The Husbandmen with high-rais'd banks secure
Their greedy hopes, and this he can endure.
But if with Bays and Dams they strive to force
His channel to a new, or narrow course;
355   No longer then within his banks he dwells,
First to a Torrent, then a Deluge swells:
Stronger, and fiercer by restraint he roars,
And knows no bound, but makes his power his shores.

333 *to the same Center move:* i.e. move concentrically, are governed by a common purpose and common principles.

339 *give themselves away:* betray themselves.

341–2 If these lines are a quotation, I have been unable to trace their source. But they are very much in Denham's own compact style, and the quotation marks probably serve only to indicate that the poet is switching to a proverb-like generalisation.

353 *Bays:* embankments.

358 The river is bounded only by the quantity of water it has to spread over the land.

Anne, Countess of Winchilsea

A NOCTURNAL RÊVERIE

LADY WINCHILSEA (1661–1720), after a brief period at the court of James II, retired with her husband to Eastwell Park, near Hythe, and found that the natural beauty of the place inspired in her "soft and Poeticall immaginations":

> Like mighty Denham's, then, methinks my hand,
> Might bid the Landskip, in strong numbers stand,
> Fix all its charms, with a Poetick skill,
> And raise its Fame above his Cooper's Hill.

She wrote chiefly to please her friends and acquaintances, but was also concerned to show that "Women are Education and not Nature's Fools", so that her isolation from critical circles did not lead to slovenly writing, but probably helped her to maintain and develop her individuality, a quality she consciously cultivated:

> Whilst in the Muses' Paths I stray,
> Whilst in their Groves, and by their secret Springs
> My Hand delights to trace unusual Things,
> And deviates from the known, and common way;
> Nor will in fading Silks compose
> Faintly th' inimitable Rose.

She did not always write as well as that, though she wrote well enough to win the approval of such men as Swift and Rowe. Few of her poems were published until the *Miscellany Poems on Several Occasions* (1713) from which the text below is taken.

The "Nocturnal Rêverie", with its placid movement and exact natural imagery, is a fresh and direct evocation of falling night, given unobtrusive shaping by the repeated phrase "In such a night" at the beginning (perhaps suggested by the similar use of the same phrase in *The Merchant of Venice*, v, i), which leads to the succession of glimpses of the scene introduced by "When" and "Whilst", and is recalled at the close. The poem was a favourite of Wordsworth's, who found her style "often admirable, chaste, tender and vigorous", and described her as a poetess "to whose writings I am especially partial".

In such a Night, when every louder Wind
Is to its distant Cavern safe confin'd;
And only gentle Zephyr fans his Wings,
And lonely Philomel, still waking, sings;
5 Or from some Tree, fam'd for the Owl's delight,
She, hollowing clear, directs the Wand'rer right:
In such a Night, when passing Clouds give place,
Or thinly vail the Heav'n's mysterious Face;
When in some River, overhung with Green,
10 The waving Moon and trembling Leaves are seen;
When freshen'd Grass now bears it self upright,
And makes cool Banks to pleasing Rest invite,
Whence springs the Woodbind, and the Bramble-Rose,
And where the sleepy Cowslip shelter'd grows;
15 Whilst now a paler Hue the Foxglove takes,
Yet checquers still with Red the dusky brakes:
When scatter'd Glow-worms, but in Twilight fine,
Shew trivial Beauties watch their Hour to shine;
Whilst Salisb'ry stands the Test of every Light,
20 In perfect Charms, and perfect Virtue bright:
When Odours, which declin'd repelling Day,
Thro' temp'rate Air uninterrupted stray;

2 *Cavern:* the mythical Cave of the Winds, from which they were released by their god, Aeolus.

3 *Zephyr:* the god of the west wind.

4 *Philomel:* the nightingale.

7 *give place:* succeed each other.

14 *sleepy Cowslip:* presumably a reference to the flower's posture. Cf. Milton's "With Cowslips wan that hang the pensive head" (*Lycidas* l. 147).

16 *checquers:* diversifies with blobs of colour (*or* light and shade).   *brakes:* thickets.

17 *but:* only.

18 *Shew:* present an image of the way in which women of moderate appearance wait for a suitable light to make the most of their looks.

19 *Salisb'ry:* Almost certainly this is Anne Tufton, who married the Earl of Salisbury in 1708/9. She would have been between sixteen and twenty when the poem was written. Her elder sister, Catherine, was Lady Winchilsea's dearest friend, and was celebrated in verse as Serena.

When darken'd Groves their softest Shadows wear,
And falling Waters we distinctly hear;
25 When thro' the Gloom more venerable shows
Some ancient Fabrick, awful in Repose,
While Sunburnt Hills their swarthy Looks conceal,
And swelling Haycocks thicken up the Vale:
When the loos'd Horse now, as his Pasture leads,
30 Comes slowly grazing thro' th' adjoining Meads,
Whose stealing Pace, and lengthen'd Shade we fear,
Till torn up Forage in his Teeth we hear:
When nibbling Sheep at large pursue their Food,
And unmolested Kine rechew the Cud;
35 When Curlews cry beneath the Village-walls,
And to her straggling brood the Partridge calls;
Their short-liv'd Jubilee the Creatures keep,
Which but endures, whilst Tyrant-Man do's sleep:
When a sedate Content the Spirit feels,
40 And no fierce Light disturbs, whilst it reveals;
But silent Musings urge the Mind to seek
Something, too high for Syllables to speak;
Till the free Soul to a compos'dness charm'd,
Finding the Elements of Rage disarm'd,
45 O'er all below a solemn Quiet grown,
Joys in th' inferiour World and thinks it like her Own:
In such a Night let Me abroad remain,
Till Morning breaks, and All's confus'd again;
Our Cares, our Toils, our Clamours are renew'd,
50 Or Pleasures, seldom reach'd, again pursu'd.

27 *swarthy:* scorched brown. (In other contexts the word can mean "grassy, covered with greensward or swarth".)

28 *swelling:* The heaps of hay seem to thicken as their shapes merge with their shadows in the darkening valley.

37 *Jubilee:* a time of rejoicing, but, more particularly, a time of remission or release from slavery.

46 *inferiour:* (i) the "lower" world, i.e. beneath the heavens, and (ii) the natural world, inferior to the world of the soul.

47 *abroad:* out of doors.

Alexander Pope

WINDSOR-FOREST

To the Right Honourable
George Lord Lansdown

Non iniussa cano: Te nostrae, Vare, Myricae
Te Nemus omne canet; nec Phoebo gratior ulla est
Quam sibi quae Vari praescripsit Pagina nomen.

Virg.[1]

JUST over two-thirds of *Windsor-Forest* was originally written some six or seven years before the conclusion celebrating the Treaty of Utrecht; but when Pope completed the poem in 1712 he clearly re-thought and re-wrote it as a whole, so that the political matters arise as naturally out of the descriptions as in his models—Virgil's *Georgics* and Denham's *Cooper's Hill*. Of the latter poem the "distinguishing Excellence" was, according to Pope, the way in which "the Descriptions of Places, and Images rais'd by the Poet, are still tending to some Hint, or leading into some Reflection, upon moral Life or political Institution: Much in the same manner as the real Sight of such Scenes and Prospects is apt to give the Mind a compos'd Turn, and incline it to Thoughts and Contemplations that have a Relation to the Object' (*Iliad*, xvi, 466 *n*.). Similarities in the setting, the historical materials and the observations confirm Pope's indebtedness to Denham, but he goes beyond his model. While Denham is "majestick" and "lofty", Pope is lively, more varied and sensuous, possessed of superior imaginative and verbal richness. There is nothing in *Cooper's Hill* so beautifully evocative as "Strait a short Thunder breaks the frozen Sky", so finely imagined as the devastated New Forest, so vivid as the description of the birds and fishes. Denham's poem has the coherence of well-managed argument: Pope's is a complex of inter-relating parts. The creation of the world from Chaos, introduced in the opening lines to define the aesthetic principle of

[1] The epigraph is from Virgil's sixth *Eclogue*, ll. 9–12 (the second part of l. 9 and the first part of l. 10 have been omitted by Pope as not being to his purpose): "I do not sing what I have not been bidden to sing. Our tamarisks and the whole woodland shall celebrate you, Varus. Nor is any page more pleasing to Phoebus than one with the name of Varus written at its head."

the landscape, is recalled by the fiat, "Let Discord cease!", which brings an end to civil war, and extends from internal politics to a vision of universal peace in the reference to Jove's banishing of Discord. The hunting theme, sounded first in the account of the Norman hunters whose "Prey was Man", is repeated in the description of the seasonable occupations of the peaceful countryside, leads to the comparison between Diana and Queen Anne, thence to the fable of Lodona, the huntress who became the hunted, and finally to the picture of the Thames Valley, where

> The shady Empire shall retain no trace
> Of War or Blood, but in the Sylvan Chace.

As the landscape is related to its past, present, and future roles in English history, and placed in a context of universal history extending from the Creation to a coming Golden Age, so the poem itself by echo, allusion and direct reference is related to both classical and English poetic traditions. It is a poem which is not understood until the reader apprehends the cunning blend of diverse materials, the subtle transitions, which make it an illustration of its own aesthetic creed:

> Where Order in Variety we see,
> And where, tho' all things differ, all agree.

The text is that of the first edition (1713) save for the addition of full-stops in ll. 50, 264, and 318, the closing of the inverted commas in l. 200, and the replacement of a full-stop by a comma in l. 322. The notes are indebted to E. Audra and Aubrey Williams, the editors of the volume, *Pastoral Poetry and An Essay on Criticism*, in the Twickenham edition of the *Poems of Alexander Pope* (1961).

> Thy Forests, Windsor! and thy green Retreats,
> At once the Monarch's and the Muse's Seats,
> Invite my Lays. Be present, Sylvan Maids!
> Unlock your Springs, and open all your Shades.
> 5   Granville commands: Your Aid O Muses bring!
> What Muse for Granville can refuse to sing?

1–2 This opening couplet, referring to the rural, national and literary aspects of the scene, introduces the three main concerns of the poem.

3 *Sylvan Maids:* The Muses, already described as dwellers in the forest, are asked to let their springs flow and allow access to their sacred groves, i.e. to inspire the poet.

5 *Granville:* George Granville, Lord Lansdown, himself a poet, had

    The Groves of Eden, vanish'd now so long,
Live in Description, and look green in Song:
These, were my Breast inspir'd with equal Flame,
10 Like them in Beauty, should be like in Fame.
Here Hills and Vales, the Woodland and the Plain,
Here Earth and Water seem to strive again,
Not Chaos-like together crush'd and bruis'd,
But as the World, harmoniously confus'd:
15 Where Order in Variety we see,
And where, tho' all things differ, all agree.
Here waving Groves a checquer'd Scene display,
And part admit and part exclude the Day;
As some coy Nymph her Lover's warm Address
20 Nor quite indulges, nor can quite repress.
There, interspers'd in Lawns and opening Glades,
Thin Trees arise that shun each other's Shades.
Here in full Light the russet Plains extend;
There wrapt in Clouds the blueish Hills ascend:
25 Ev'n the wild Heath displays her Purple Dies,
And 'midst the Desart fruitful Fields arise,
That crown'd with tufted Trees and springing Corn,
Like verdant Isles the sable Waste adorn.

urged Pope to publish *Windsor-Forest*: hence the epigraph, *non iniussa cano*.
He was a member of the Tory government engaged in 1713 on the final
negotiations preceding the Treaty of Utrecht, which concluded the peace
celebrated at the end of the poem.

   7–10 Pope is saying that, had he Milton's genius, Windsor-Forest would
be immortalised, as Eden was in *Paradise Lost*. Cf. *Cooper's Hill*, p. 27,
ll. 71–2.

   13 *Chaos-like:* refers to the notion that prior to the Creation the elements
clashed in Chaos. Creation blended them together in harmony. See *Cooper's
Hill*, p. 32, ll. 205–6 n.

   17 *checquer'd:* with variations of light and shade.

   21 *Lawns:* grassy spaces between trees, glades.   **26** *Desart:* barren land

   27 *tufted Trees:* trees clustered in groups (in contrast to those described
in l. 22).

   28 *sable:* The contrast with "verdant" suggests that the colour *sable*
(between black and brown) is intended, but Pope may be thinking of the
sandy top-soil in these waste areas. Cf. l. 88, and French, *sable*.

Let India boast her Plants, nor envy we
30   The weeping Amber or the balmy Tree,
While by our Oaks the precious Loads are born,
And Realms commanded which those Trees adorn.
Not proud Olympus yields a nobler Sight,
Tho' Gods assembled grace his tow'ring Height,
35   Than what more humble Mountains offer here,
Where, in their Blessings, all those Gods appear.
See Pan with Flocks, with Fruits Pomona crown'd,
Here blushing Flora paints th' enamel'd Ground,
Here Ceres' Gifts in waving Prospect stand,
40   And nodding tempt the joyful Reaper's Hand,
Rich Industry sits smiling on the Plains,
And Peace and Plenty tell, a STUART reigns.

Not thus the Land appear'd in Ages past,
A dreary Desart and a gloomy Waste,
45   To Savage Beasts and Savage Laws a Prey,

30 *Amber . . . balmy Tree:* Both amber and balm are exuded from trees.
See l. 391 *n.*

31 *Oaks:* ships built of oak.

33 *Olympus:* a mountain in Greece, the home of the Gods.

35 *humble:* low, and lowly. *Mountains,* here and elsewhere, can mean "hills".

36 *their Blessings:* Although the Gods cannot be seen at Windsor, they
are manifest in their gifts.

37-9 *Pan, Pomona, Flora, Ceres:* the god of flocks and herds, and the god-
desses of fruit, flowers, and corn, respectively.

38 *enamel'd:* Metals were covered with a coating of enamel as a "ground"
on which enamel colours could be painted. Johnson's *Dictionary* defines
"enamel" as "To inlay; to variegate with colours".

41 *Industry:* agriculture.

42 STUART: Queen Anne, daughter of James II. *Stuart* is emphasised by
capitalisation because, as some critics have pointed out, the following attack
on the Norman Kings probably has some reference to William III, whose
reign had been a break in the Stuart dynasty (although his wife, Mary,
with whom he shared the sovereignty, was also a daughter of James II).

45 *Savage Laws:* "The Forest Laws." (*Pope, 1713.*) Windsor Forest, like
the New Forest, was a royal hunting preserve, the word "forest" deriving
from the fact that these areas were outside (Latin, *foris*) the ordinary laws
of the kingdom.

And Kings more furious and severe than they:
Who claim'd the Skies, dispeopled Air and Floods,
The lonely Lords of empty Wilds and Woods.
Cities laid waste, they storm'd the Dens and Caves
50 (For wiser Brutes were backward to be Slaves).
What could be free, when lawless Beasts obey'd,
And ev'n the Elements a Tyrant sway'd?
In vain kind Seasons swell'd the teeming Grain,
Soft show'rs distill'd, and Suns grew warm in vain;
55 The Swain with Tears to Beasts his Labour yields,
And famish'd dies amidst his ripen'd Fields.
No wonder Savages or Subjects slain
Were equal Crimes in a Despotick Reign;
Both doom'd alike for sportive Tyrants bled,
60 But Subjects starv'd while Savages were fed.
Proud Nimrod first the bloody Chace began,
A mighty Hunter, and his Prey was Man.
Our haughty Norman boasts that barb'rous Name,
And makes his trembling Slaves the Royal Game.
65 The Fields are ravish'd from th' industrious Swains,
From Men their Cities, and from Gods their Fanes:

46 *Kings:* William the Conqueror and William Rufus. Their ruthless creation of hunting preserves and game-laws made them familiar examples of tyranny.

47 *claim'd the Skies:* The Normans' assertion of game-rights is seen as a tyrannous claim of authority over the very skies.

53–6 The protected game-birds and animals devoured the crops.

57 *Savages:* wild beasts. In 1736 Pope amended line 57 to "What wonder then, a beast or subject slain", and line 60 to "But that the subject starv'd, the beast was fed", on the grounds that "the word Savages is not so properly apply'd to beasts as to men".

61 *Nimrod:* according to *Genesis,* x, 9, "a mighty hunter before the Lord". Bible commentaries represented him as a type of the tyrant.

64 *Game:* means both "sport" and "creatures which are hunted". Cf. "Sport" in l. 78.

65 *The Fields:* "Alluding to the New Forest, and the Tyrannies exercis'd there by William the First." (*Pope, 1713.*)

66 *Fanes:* temples (i.e. churches).

The levell'd Towns with Weeds lie cover'd o'er,
The hollow Winds thro' naked Temples roar;
Round broken Columns clasping Ivy twin'd;
70 O'er Heaps of Ruins stalk'd the stately Hind;
The Fox obscene to gaping Tombs retires,
And Wolves with Howling fill the sacred Quires.
Aw'd by his Nobles, by his Commons curst,
Th' Oppressor rul'd Tyrannick where he *durst*,
75 Stretch'd o'er the Poor, and Church, his Iron Rod,
And treats alike his Vassals and his God.
Whom ev'n the Saxon spar'd, and bloody Dane,
The wanton Victims of his *Sport* remain.
But see the Man who spacious Regions gave
80 A Waste for Beasts, himself deny'd a Grave!
Stretch'd on the Lawn his second Hope survey,
At once the Chaser and at once the Prey.
Lo Rufus, tugging at the deadly Dart,
Bleeds in the Forest, like a wounded Hart.

68 *hollow:* i.e. hollow-sounding.

71 *obscene:* loathsome or ill-omened (a latinism).

72 *And Wolves with Howling:* In 1736 Pope substituted "And savage Howlings", because he "thought this an error, wolves not being common in England at the time of the Conqueror".   *Quires:* choirs.

78 *wanton:* The epithet really applies to *Sport*, and means "capricious", but juxtaposition with "victims" emphasises the meanings "unprovoked", "merciless", as in the phrase "wanton cruelty".

80 *deny'd a Grave:* When William I was about to be buried near Caen, the owner of the land objected and his consent had to be bought.

81 *his second Hope:* "Richard, second Son of William the Conqueror." (*Pope, 1713.*) In *The Spectator*, No. 483 (September 13, 1712), Addison had ridiculed the old historians who saw the hand of God in this: "William the Conqueror's Race generally found their Judgments in the New Forest, where their Father had pulled down Churches and Monastries." According to one historian Richard died in the New Forest by "a pestilential blast", but Pope seems to have in mind the story that he was killed by a stag which he was hunting. (For "Lawn", see note on l. 21.)

83 *Rufus:* William II was accidentally killed while hunting in the New Forest.

85   Succeeding Monarchs heard the Subjects' Cries,
     Nor saw displeas'd the peaceful Cottage rise.
     Then gath'ring Flocks on unknown Mountains fed,
     O'er sandy Wilds were yellow Harvests spread,
     The Forests wonder'd at th' unusual Grain,
90   And secret Transports touch'd the conscious Swain.
     Fair *Liberty*, Britannia's Goddess, rears
     Her chearful Head, and leads the golden Years.

     Ye vig'rous Swains! while Youth ferments your Blood,
     And purer Spirits swell the sprightly Flood,
95   Now range the Hills, the thickest Woods beset,
     Wind the shrill Horn, or spread the waving Net.
     When milder Autumn Summer's Heat succeeds,
     And in the new-shorn Field the Partridge feeds,
     Before his Lord the ready Spaniel bounds,
100 Panting with Hope, he tries the furrow'd Grounds,
     But when the tainted Gales the Game betray,
     Couch'd close he lyes, and meditates the Prey;
     Secure they trust th' unfaithful Field, beset,
     Till hov'ring o'er 'em sweeps the swelling Net.
105 Thus (if small Things we may with great compare)
     When Albion sends her eager Sons to War,

87 *unknown:* unknown to them because they had not previously been allowed to graze there.

90 *conscious:* well aware (of the change).

92 *chearful:* full of cheer, bringing good cheer.

93 *ferments your Blood:* The animal spirits were supposed to course more actively through the blood in youth and to bubble up.

94 *sprightly:* This is a play on words since "spright" is originally the same word as "spirit".

101 *the tainted Gales:* breezes carrying the scent of an animal.

102 *meditates:* fixes his attention on.

103 *Secure:* Both meanings of the word are implied: (i) "safe", and (ii) "over-confident". The word is contrasted with "unfaithful" (i.e. "treacherous").

105 *if small Things . . . compare:* an expression from Virgil's *Georgics* (iv, 176), echoed in *Paradise Lost* (ii, 921-2 and vi, 310-11).

106 *Albion:* England.

Pleas'd, in the Gen'ral's Sight, the Host lye down
Sudden, before some unsuspecting Town,
The Young, the Old, one Instant makes our Prize,
110 And high in Air Britannia's Standard flies.

See! from the Brake the whirring Pheasant springs,
And mounts exulting on triumphant Wings;
Short is his Joy! he feels the fiery Wound,
Flutters in Blood, and panting beats the Ground.
115 Ah! what avail his glossie, varying Dyes,
His Purple Crest, and Scarlet-circled Eyes,
The vivid Green his shining Plumes unfold;
His painted Wings, and Breast that flames with Gold?

Nor yet, when moist Arcturus clouds the Sky,
120 The Woods and Fields their pleasing Toils deny.
To Plains with well-breath'd Beagles we repair,
And trace the Mazes of the circling Hare.
(Beasts, taught by us, their Fellow Beasts pursue,
And learn of Man each other to undo.)
125 With slaught'ring Guns th' unweary'd Fowler roves,
When Frosts have whiten'd all the naked Groves;
Where Doves in Flocks the leafless Trees o'ershade,
And lonely Woodcocks haunt the watry Glade.
He lifts the Tube, and levels with his Eye;
130 Strait a short Thunder breaks the frozen Sky.
Oft, as in Airy Rings they skim the Heath,
The clam'rous Plovers feel the Leaden Death:
Oft as the mounting Larks their Notes prepare,
They fall, and leave their little Lives in Air.

119 *Arcturus:* In September, when the star Arcturus (in the constellation Boötes) rises with the sun, it was supposed to bring a spell of wet weather.
121 *well-breath'd:* with good lungs, strong in the wind.
130 *Strait:* at once.   *breaks the frozen Sky:* Pope imagines a low, grey sky like a sheet of ice which shatters at the brief reverberation of the gun.
132 *Plovers:* later amended to "Lapwings". Lapwings belong to the plover family, and Pope probably felt that the emendation was a gain in accuracy.

135 In genial Spring, beneath the quiv'ring Shade
  Where cooling Vapours breathe along the Mead,
  The patient Fisher takes his silent Stand
  Intent, his Angle trembling in his Hand;
  With Looks unmov'd, he hopes the Scaly Breed,
140 And eyes the dancing Cork and bending Reed.
  Our plenteous Streams a various Race supply;
  The bright-ey'd Perch with Fins of Tyrian Dye,
  The silver Eel, in shining Volumes roll'd,
  The yellow Carp, in Scales bedrop'd with Gold,
145 Swift Trouts, diversify'd with Crimson Stains,
  And Pykes, the Tyrants of the watry Plains.

  Now Cancer glows with Phœbus' fiery Car;
  The Youth rush eager to the Sylvan War;
  Swarm o'er the Lawns, the Forest Walks surround,
150 Rowze the fleet Hart, and chear the opening Hound.
  Th' impatient Courser pants in ev'ry Vein,
  And pawing, seems to beat the distant Plain,
  Hills, Vales, and Floods appear already crost,
  And ere he starts, a thousand Steps are lost.
155 See! the bold Youth strain up the threatning Steep,
  Rush thro' the Thickets, down the Vallies sweep,

139 *hopes:* hopes for, hopes to catch.

142 *Tyrian dye:* The noble purple dye was made from murex, a shell-fish, gathered and prepared at Tyre, but, in eighteenth-century poetry, "purple" was often, as here, equated with "red". (See Johnson's *Dictionary*.)

143 *Volumes:* convolutions, coils.

147 *Cancer:* the constellation that rises with the sun in June and July. *Phœbus' fiery Car:* Phœbus, the sun-god, was supposed to drive the chariot of the sun across the sky.

148 *Sylvan:* woodland.

149 *Walks:* divisions of a forest.

150 *Rowze:* make deer leave their shelter (a hunting term). *opening:* giving tongue, crying out in pursuit.

151 *pants:* throbs. (The word does not necessarily refer to breathing.)

154 The horse tires himself with pawing the air before he starts.

155 *Youth:* (plural; as in l. 148.)

Hang o'er their Coursers' Heads with eager Speed,
And Earth rolls back beneath the flying Steed.
Let old Arcadia boast her spacious Plain,
160   Th' Immortal Huntress, and her Virgin Train;
Nor envy Windsor! since thy Shades have seen
As bright a Goddess, and as chast a Queen;
Whose Care, like hers, protects the Sylvan Reign,
The Earth's fair Light, and Empress of the Main.

165   Here, as old Bards have sung, Diana stray'd,
Bath'd in the Springs, or sought the cooling Shade;
Here arm'd with Silver Bows, in early Dawn,
Her buskin'd Virgins trac'd the Dewy Lawn.
Above the rest a rural Nymph was fam'd,
170   Thy Offspring, Thames! the fair Lodona nam'd,
(Lodona's Fate, in long Oblivion cast,
The Muse shall sing, and what she sings shall last)
Scarce could the Goddess from her Nymph be known,
But by the Crescent and the golden Zone,
175   She scorn'd the Praise of Beauty, and the Care;
A belt her Waste, a Fillet binds her Hair,

159 *Arcadia:* a district in Greece traditionally famous for pastoral peace and richness.

160 *Th' Immortal Huntress:* Diana, goddess of hunting and of chastity, was accompanied by a company of virgins.

161 *Nor envy Windsor!:* an imperative addressed to Windsor, which should not envy Arcadia, since Queen Anne was as fair and chaste as Diana. The allusion is not disturbed by the Queen's numerous but short-lived children.

163-4 Diana was not only goddess of hunting and chastity, but also of the moon and thus controlled the tides. Queen Anne, also fond of hunting, was the light of the earth in beauty, and, as Queen of England, ruled the waves.

167 *Silver Bows:* As huntress and moon-goddess, Diana had a silver bow as her weapon.

168 *buskin'd:* wearing buskins, a kind of high boot.   *trac'd:* trod, moved across.   **170** *Lodona:* See l. 205 n.

174 *the Crescent and the golden Zone:* Diana's insignia were a crescent moon and a golden girdle.

176 *Fillet:* a narrow head-band.

A painted Quiver on her Shoulder sounds,
And with her Dart the flying Deer she wounds.
It chanc'd, as eager of the Chace the Maid
180 Beyond the Forest's verdant Limits stray'd,
Pan saw and lov'd, and furious with Desire
Pursu'd her Flight; her Flight increas'd his Fire.
Not half so swift the trembling Doves can fly,
When the fierce Eagle cleaves the liquid Sky;
185 Not half so swiftly the fierce Eagle moves,
When thro' the Clouds he drives the trembling Doves;
As from the God with fearful speed she flew,
As did the God with equal Speed pursue.
Now fainting, sinking, pale, the Nymph appears;
190 Now close behind his sounding Steps she hears;
And now his Shadow reach'd her as she run,
(His Shadow lengthen'd by the setting Sun)
And now his shorter Breath with sultry Air
Pants on her Neck, and fans her parting Hair.
195 In vain on Father Thames she calls for Aid,
Nor could Diana help her injur'd Maid.
Faint, breathless, thus she pray'd, nor pray'd in vain;
"Ah Cynthia! ah—tho' banish'd from thy Train,
"Let me, O let me, to the Shades repair,
200 "My native Shades—there weep, and murmur there."
She said, and melting as in Tears she lay,
In a soft, silver Stream dissolv'd away.
The silver Stream her Virgin Coldness keeps,
For ever murmurs, and for ever weeps;
205 Still bears the Name the hapless Virgin bore,
And bathes the Forest where she rang'd before.

177 *sounds:* i.e. as it bounces when she runs.
181 *Pan:* nature-god of pastures, forests, flocks and herds.
182 *Fire:* passion.
184 *liquid:* clear, transparent (from Latin *liquidus*).
199 *Shades:* "To repair to the Shades" was to die and join the spirits of the dead. But Lodona adds *My native Shades* and thus brings in the suggestion of a shady valley, through which the stream runs.
205 *Name:* "The River Loddon." (*Pope, 1713.*) The Loddon is a tributary of the Thames.

In her chast Current oft the Goddess laves,
And with Celestial Tears augments the Waves.
Oft in her Glass the musing Shepherd spies
210 The headlong Mountains and the downward Skies,
The watry Landskip of the pendant Woods,
And absent Trees that tremble in the Floods;
In the clear azure Gleam the Flocks are seen,
And floating Forests paint the Waves with Green.
215 Thro' the fair Scene rowl slow the lingring Streams,
Then foaming pour along, and rush into the Thames.

Thou too, great Father of the British Floods!
With joyful Pride survey'st our lofty Woods,
Where tow'ring Oaks their spreading Honours rear,
220 And future Navies on thy Banks appear.
Not Neptune's self from all his Floods receives
A wealthier Tribute, than to thine he gives.
No Seas so rich, so full no Streams appear,
No Lake so gentle, and no Spring so clear.
225 Not fabled Po more swells the Poet's Lays,
While thro' the Skies his shining Current strays,
Than thine, which visits Windsor's fam'd Abodes,
To grace the Mansion of our earthly Gods.
Nor all his Stars a brighter Lustre show,
230 Than the fair Nymphs that gild thy Shore below:

217 *great Father:* the river Thames.

219 *Honours:* branches and foliage. (The hair was often called the "honours" of the head. Cf. "crowning glory".)

221 *Neptune's self:* the sea-god; hence, the ocean.

222 *than to thine he gives:* because he brings the world's commerce to the Thames.

225 *fabled Po:* The river Po was called by the Greeks, Eridanus, also the name of a constellation of a long, winding shape. Cf. *Cooper's Hill*, p. 32, l. 193 *n.*

227 *Than thine:* The Thames had been celebrated by many poets including Spenser and Denham.

228 *earthly Gods:* monarchs.

230 *gild:* adorn.

Here Jove himself, subdu'd by Beauty still,
Might change Olympus for a nobler Hill.

    Happy the Man whom this bright Court approves,
His Sov'reign favours, and his Country loves;
235 Happy next him who to these Shades retires,
Whom Nature charms, and whom the Muse inspires,
Whom humbler Joys of home-felt Quiet please,
Successive Study, Exercise and Ease.
He gathers Health from Herbs the Forest yields,
240 And of their fragrant Physick spoils the Fields:
With Chymic Art exalts the Min'ral Pow'rs,
And draws the Aromatick Souls of Flow'rs.
Now marks the Course of rolling Orbs on high;
O'er figur'd Worlds now travels with his Eye.
245 Of ancient Writ unlocks the learned Store,
Consults the Dead, and lives past Ages o'er,
Or wandring thoughtful in the silent Wood,
Attends the Duties of the Wise and Good,
T' observe a Mean, be to himself a Friend,
250 To follow Nature, and regard his End.

231 Jove, the ruler of the gods, was notoriously susceptible to beauty.

232 *a nobler Hill:* the hill on which Windsor Castle stands.

233 *Happy the Man:* an expression, taken from Virgil's *Georgics* (ii, 458) and Horace's *Epode* ii, frequently used in late seventeenth- and early eighteenth-century poems of rural retirement.

233 ff. The happy courtier is probably Granville; the happy retirer to the country, Sir William Trumbull. See l. 256 *n.*

238 *Successive:* in turn.

240 *Physick:* medicine.

241 *exalts:* extracts the essence of, refines (a term from alchemy).

242 *draws:* distils (i.e. draws out) essences of perfumes.

244 *figur'd Worlds:* The Twickenham editor suggests "Perhaps the Zodiac or a globe of the world". It may mean, in contrast to the preceding line, that Trumbull turns from the stars to the study of maps of the world.

249 *T' observe a Mean:* to follow the Stoic principle of avoiding extremes.

250 i.e. to live in harmony with the natural world and fundamental human nature, and to remember mortality.

Or looks on Heav'n with more than mortal Eyes,
Bids his free Soul expatiate in the Skies,
Amidst her Kindred Stars familiar roam,
Survey the Region, and confess her Home!
255   Such was the Life great Scipio once admir'd,
Thus Atticus, and Trumbal thus retir'd.

Ye sacred Nine! that all my Soul possess,
Whose Raptures fire me, and whose Visions bless,
Bear me, oh bear me to sequester'd Scenes
260   Of Bow'ry Mazes and surrounding Greens;
To Thames's Banks which fragrant Breezes fill,
Or where ye Muses sport on Cooper's Hill.
(On Cooper's Hill eternal Wreaths shall grow,
While lasts the Mountain, or while Thames shall flow.)
265   I seem thro' consecrated Walks to rove,
And hear soft Musick dye along the Grove;
Led by the Sound I roam from Shade to Shade,
By God-like Poets Venerable made:
Here his first Lays Majestick Denham sung;
270   There the last Numbers flow'd from Cowley's Tongue.

251 *with more than mortal Eyes:* spiritually.

252 *expatiate:* wander freely in space.

254 *confess:* acknowledge, recognise.

255 *Scipio:* Scipio Africanus, after his defeat of Carthage, withdrew to his country home.

256 *Atticus:* Titus Pomponius, Cicero's friend, avoided political involvement and withdrew to pursue his studies at Athens—hence the name Atticus.   *Trumbal:* Sir William Trumbull, a politician and statesman of some importance in the reign of William III, retired from public life to Easthampstead Park. He was a neighbour of the Pope family (living at Binfield in Windsor Forest), who encouraged the young poet, and suggested the subject of this poem.

257 *Ye sacred Nine!:* the nine Muses.

269 *Denham:* Here Pope acknowledges his debt to *Cooper's Hill.* Denham was living at Egham, near Windsor, when he wrote his early poems.

270 *Cowley:* "Mr. Cowley died at Chertsey on the Borders of the Forest, and was from thence convey'd to Westminster." (*Pope, 1713.*) Cowley's reputation as a poet was still very high in the early eighteenth century. He died in 1667, aged 49.

O early lost! what Tears the River shed
When the sad Pomp along his Banks was led?
His drooping Swans on ev'ry Note expire,
And on his Willows hung each Muse's Lyre.

275   Since Fate relentless stop'd their Heav'nly Voice,
No more the Forests ring, or Groves rejoice;
Who now shall charm the Shades where Cowley strung
His living Harp, and lofty Denham sung?
But hark! the Groves rejoice, the Forest rings!
280   Are these reviv'd? or is it Granville sings?

'Tis yours, my Lord, to bless our soft Retreats,
And call the Muses to their ancient Seats,
To paint anew the flow'ry Sylvan Scenes,
To crown the Forests with Immortal Greens,
285   Make Windsor Hills in lofty Numbers rise,
And lift her Turrets nearer to the Skies;
To sing those Honours you deserve to wear,
And add new Lustre to her Silver *Star*.

Here noble Surrey felt the sacred Rage,

272 *sad Pomp:* Cowley's body was conveyed down river to Westminster
with great ceremony. Johnson's *Dictionary* gives as one meaning of "pomp",
"a procession of splendour and ostentation".

273 *Swans:* A rather strained attempt to refer to the popular belief that
swans sang before they died.

274 The reference is to Psalm cxxxvii, where the Jews in captivity hang
their harps upon the willows to show that their grief is too great for them
to sing.   *Each Muse* is involved because Cowley practised (or is supposed
to have practised) all the various kinds of poetry.

280 *Granville sings:* in his *Poems Upon Several Occasions* (1712).

285 *Numbers:* metrical writing.

288 *Silver Star:* the Star of the Order of the Garter. Granville had
celebrated the founding of the Order at Windsor in a poem entitled *The
Progress of Beauty*. He never became a knight of the Order.

289 *Surrey:* "Henry Howard E. of Surrey, one of the first Refiners of

290   Surrey, the Granville of a former Age:
       Matchless his Pen, victorious was his Lance;
       Bold in the Lists, and graceful in the Dance:
       In the same Shades the Cupids tun'd his Lyre,
       To the same Notes, of Love, and soft Desire:
295   Fair Geraldine, bright Object of his Vow,
       Then fill'd the Groves, as heav'nly Myra now.

         Oh wou'dst thou sing what Heroes Windsor bore,
       What Kings first breath'd upon her winding Shore,
       Or raise old Warriors whose ador'd Remains
300   In weeping Vaults her hallow'd Earth contains!
       With Edward's Acts adorn the shining Page,
       Stretch his long Triumphs down thro' ev'ry Age,
       Draw Kings enchain'd; and Cressi's glorious Field,
       The Lillies blazing on the Regal Shield.
305   Then, from her Roofs when Verrio's Colours fall,
       And leave inanimate the naked Wall;
       Still in thy Song shou'd vanquish'd France appear,
       And bleed for ever under Britain's Spear.

the English Poetry; famous in the Time of Henry the VIIIth for his Sonnets, the Scene of many of which is laid at Windsor." (*Pope, 1713.*)

292 *Lists:* jousting tournaments, or, literally, the place where these were held.

295 *Fair Geraldine:* Surrey addressed one sonnet to "Geraldine", but a legend grew up of his love for Lady Elizabeth Fitzgerald. At the time the sonnet referred to was written, the lady was about 9 years old.

296 *Myra:* Granville used this name for Mary of Modena, queen of James II, and later for his mistress, Frances Brudenal.

298 *winding Shore:* Pope is thinking of the old etymology of Windsor, as meaning "winding banks or shore".

300 *weeping:* dripping with damp—used here to suggest mourning.

301 *Edward's Acts:* "Edward III. born here." (*Pope, 1713.*) For this and the next three lines, see *Cooper's Hill*, p. 27, ll. 77 ff.

305 *Verrio:* Antonio Verrio had painted in St. George's Hall, Windsor, the scene after the battle of Crecy when the Black Prince led King John of France captive, and various other painted ceilings at Windsor were his work.

306 *inanimate:* lifeless, without representations of living figures.

Let softer Strains Ill-fated Henry mourn,
310 And Palms Eternal flourish round his Urn.
Here o'er the Martyr-King the Marble weeps,
And fast beside him, once-fear'd Edward sleeps:
Whom not th' extended Albion could contain,
From old Belerium to the German Main,
315 The Grave unites; where ev'n the Great find Rest,
And blended lie th' Oppressor and th' Opprest!

Make sacred Charles's Tomb for ever known,
(Obscure the Place, and uninscrib'd the Stone).
Oh Fact accurst! What Tears has Albion shed,
320 Heav'ns! what new Wounds, and how her old have bled?
She saw her Sons with purple Deaths expire,
Her sacred Domes involv'd in rolling Fire,
A dreadful Series of Intestine Wars,
Inglorious Triumphs, and dishonest Scars.
325 At length great ANNA said—Let Discord cease!
She said, the World obey'd, and all was *Peace*!

309 *Henry:* "Henry VI." (*Pope, 1713.*) Buried in St. George's Chapel, Windsor.

310 *Palms Eternal:* These are palms appropriate to martyrs. After his death many miracles were attributed to him.

312 *Edward:* "Edward IV." (*Pope, 1713.*) The enemy and supplanter of Henry VI is also buried in St. George's Chapel.

314 *Belerium:* Land's End.   *German Main:* the North Sea.

317 *Charles's Tomb:* Charles I was hurriedly buried in the same tomb as Henry VIII in St. George's Chapel. Plans were made for a monument but were never implemented.

319 *Fact:* crime.

321-4 The Great Plague (1665), the Fire of London (1666), the Monmouth Rising, and the Revolution of 1688, are all seen as divine punishments for the execution of Charles I.

321 *purple Deaths:* Purple pustules were symptomatic of the bubonic plague.

322 *sacred Domes:* churches, domed or not.

324 *dishonest Scars: Dishonest* means "shameful, dishonourable": scars were usually thought of as marks of honour.

325 *Anna:* Pope is deliberately echoing the language of the Creation. The intestine wars were ended by Queen Anne's being both a Stuart and a

In that blest Moment, from his Oozy Bed
Old Father Thames advanc'd his rev'rend Head.
His Tresses dropt with Dews, and o'er the Stream
330   His shining Horns diffus'd a golden Gleam:
Grav'd on his Urn appear'd the Moon, that guides
His swelling Waters, and alternate Tydes;
The figur'd Streams in Waves of Silver roll'd,
And on their Banks Augusta rose in Gold.
335   Around his Throne the Sea-born Brothers stood,
That swell with Tributary Urns his Flood.
First the fam'd Authors of his ancient Name,
The winding Isis, and the fruitful Tame:
The Kennet swift, for silver Eels renown'd;
340   The Loddon slow, with verdant Alders crown'd:
Cole, whose clear Streams his flow'ry Islands lave;
And chalky Wey, that rolls a milky Wave:
The blue, transparent Vandalis appears;
The gulphy Lee his sedgy Tresses rears:
345   And sullen Mole, that hides his diving Flood;
And silent Darent, stain'd with Danish Blood.

Protestant successor to William and Mary, and by the union with Scotland (1707). This poem was occasioned by the concluding stages of the Treaty of Utrecht, which brought peace to Europe after the long wars.

328 *advanc'd:* raised up.

330 *Horns:* River-gods traditionally had the horns of a bull, and carried urns.

333 *figur'd Streams:* "shaped into a figure, represented by figures" (O.E.D.), parallel to "Grav'd". Cf. l. 244 *n.*

334 *Augusta:* London. (Cf. *Trivia* p. 69, l. 145.)

335 *Sea-born:* See *Cooper's Hill*, p. 30, l. 161 *n.*

337 The name, *Tamesis*, was supposed to be a combination of the names of the Thame and the Isis.

341 *Cole:* the river Colne.

343 *Vandalis:* the river Wandle.

344 *gulphy:* full of eddies. (It seems unlikely that the other sense, "abysmally deep", is intended.)

345 *sullen Mole:* The river Mole runs underground at Burford Bridge near Dorking.

346 At Otford, on the river Darenth, the Danes were bloodily defeated by the Saxons in 1016.

     High in the midst, upon his Urn reclin'd,
     (His Sea-green Mantle waving with the Wind)
     The God appear'd; he turn'd his azure Eyes
350 Where Windsor-Domes and pompous Turrets rise,
     Then bow'd and spoke; the Winds forget to roar,
     And the hush'd Waves glide softly to the Shore.

     Hail Sacred *Peace*! hail long-expected Days,
     That Thames's Glory to the Stars shall raise!
355 Tho' Tyber's Streams immortal Rome behold,
     Tho' foaming Hermus swells with Tydes of Gold,
     From Heav'n it self tho' sev'nfold Nilus flows,
     And Harvests on a hundred Realms bestows;
     These now no more shall be the Muse's Themes,
360 Lost in my Fame, as in the Sea their Streams.
     Let Volga's Banks with Iron Squadrons shine,
     And Groves of Lances glitter on the Rhine,
     Let barb'rous Ganges arm a servile Train;
     Be mine the Blessings of a peaceful Reign.
365 No more my Sons shall dye with British Blood
     Red Iber's Sands, or Ister's foaming Flood;
     Safe on my Shore each unmolested Swain
     Shall tend the Flocks, or reap the bearded Grain;
     The shady Empire shall retain no Trace
370 Of War or Blood, but in the Sylvan Chace,

350 *pompous:* magnificent.

353 *Hail Sacred Peace!:* The Treaty of Utrecht, finally signed in April 1713, followed negotiations begun in October 1711, and ended the war of the Spanish Succession which began in 1701.   *long-expected:* long awaited.

356 *Hermus:* See *Cooper's Hill*, p. 31, ll. 165–6 *n*.

357 According to Herodotus the Nile flowed into the Mediterranean through five natural and two artificial mouths. Its source was unknown.

361 This refers to the wars of Charles XII of Sweden against Russia. The Rhine and Ganges had also been the scenes of recent wars.

366 *Iber:* the river Ebro. English troops had campaigned in Spain in 1710. *Ister's foaming Flood:* the Danube. The great battle of Blenheim was fought near the Danube in 1704.

     The Trumpets sleep, while chearful Horns are blown,
     And Arms employ'd on Birds and Beasts alone.
     Behold! th' ascending Villas on my Side
     Project long Shadows o'er the Chrystal Tyde.
375 Behold! Augusta's glitt'ring Spires increase,
     And Temples rise, the beauteous Works of Peace.
     I see, I see where two fair Cities bend
     Their ample Bow, a new White-Hall ascend!
     There mighty Nations shall inquire their Doom,
380 The World's great Oracle in Times to come;
     There Kings shall sue, and suppliant States be seen
     Once more to bend before a British QUEEN.

       Thy Trees, fair Windsor! now shall leave their Woods,
     And half thy Forests rush into my Floods,
385 Bear Britain's Thunder, and her Cross display,
     To the bright Regions of the rising Day;
     Tempt Icy Seas, where scarce the Waters roll,
     Where clearer Flames glow round the frozen Pole;
     Or under Southern Skies exalt their Sails,
390 Led by new Stars, and born by spicy Gales!
     For me the Balm shall bleed, and Amber flow,
     The Coral redden, and the Ruby glow,

373 *Villas:* The banks of the Thames were a favourite site for splendid country-houses.

376 *Temples rise:* In Queen Anne's reign fifty new churches were built in London.

377-8 Where the cities of Westminster and London meet on the bend of the river, Whitehall, burnt down in 1698, was rebuilt.

382 *Once more:* as before Queen Elizabeth I.

384 *half thy Forests rush:* i.e. to become ships.

385 *Thunder . . . Cross:* i.e. guns and the English flag. But less specifically Pope may mean power and religion.

387 *Tempt:* venture on.

388 *clearer Flames:* Aurora Borealis.

391 *Balm shall bleed:* Balm is an aromatic resin exuded from cuts made in the bark of trees.   *Amber:* a fossilised resin, found chiefly on southern coasts of the Baltic.

The Pearly Shell its lucid Globe infold,
And Phœbus warm the ripening Ore to Gold.
395 The Time shall come, when free as Seas or Wind
Unbounded Thames shall flow for all Mankind,
Whole Nations enter with each swelling Tyde,
And Oceans join whom they did first divide;
Earth's distant Ends our Glory shall behold,
400 And the new World launch forth to seek the Old.
Then Ships of uncouth Form shall stem the Tyde,
And Feather'd People crowd my wealthy Side,
While naked Youth and painted Chiefs admire
Our Speech, our Colour, and our strange Attire!
405 Oh stretch thy Reign, fair *Peace*! from Shore to Shore,
Till Conquest cease, and Slav'ry be no more:
Till the freed Indians in their native Groves
Reap their own Fruits, and woo their Sable Loves,
Peru once more a Race of Kings behold,
410 And other Mexicos be roof'd with Gold.
Exil'd by Thee from Earth to deepest Hell,
In Brazen Bonds shall barb'rous *Discord* dwell:

394 *ripening Ore:* It was believed that the sun penetrated the earth and "ripened" minerals into gold and precious stones.

396 *Unbounded Thames:* In 1751 Pope explained this as "A wish that London may be made a FREE PORT."

401 *uncouth:* (1) unfamiliar, and (2) grotesque.   *stem the Tyde:* make headway against the tide, i.e. sail upstream against the river's flow.

402–3 In 1710 four Iroquois chiefs had visited London.

403 *admire:* wonder at.

407 *freed Indians:* American Indians, freed by the Treaty of Utrecht from Spanish rule.

408 *Sable:* dark brown.

409 *Peru:* The long Inca dynasty had ruled Peru until the coming of the Spaniards.

410 *Mexicos:* Mexico was famous for its gold, and Aztec temples were richly adorned with it.

411–12 The peace treaty would put an end to war as Jupiter had banished Discord from Heaven.

Gigantick *Pride*, pale *Terror*, gloomy *Care*,
And mad *Ambition*, shall attend her there.
415 There purple *Vengeance* bath'd in Gore retires,
Her Weapons blunted, and extinct her Fires:
There hateful *Envy* her own Snakes shall feel,
And *Persecution* mourn her broken Wheel:
There *Faction* roars, *Rebellion* bites her Chain,
420 And gasping Furies thirst for Blood in vain.

Here cease thy Flight, nor with unhallow'd Lays
Touch the fair Fame of Albion's Golden Days.
The Thoughts of Gods let Granville's Verse recite,
And bring the Scenes of opening Fate to Light.
425 My humble Muse, in unambitious Strains,
Paints the green Forests and the flow'ry Plains,
Where Peace descending bids her Olives spring,
And scatters Blessings from her Dove-like Wing.
Ev'n I more sweetly pass my careless Days,
430 Pleas'd in the silent Shade with empty Praise;
Enough for me, that to the listning Swains
First in these Fields I sung the Sylvan Strains.

417 *Envy:* Envy was imaged as deriving her venom from a diet of snakes. Here, Pope is foreseeing a time when Envy, being frustrated, will suffer from her own venom.

418 *Persecution:* Persecutors broke the bodies of their victims on the wheel. Now the wheel itself shall be broken.

419 *Faction:* turbulent political and religious parties.   *Rebellion . . . Chain:* i.e. the rebellious will be unable to do damage since they will be firmly restrained.

421-2 Pope bids his pastoral Muse to cease its visionary attempt to describe the coming Golden Age.

423 *The Thoughts of Gods:* Cf. l. 228 *n*. Granville had already celebrated James II and Mary of Modena as divinities.

429 *careless:* carefree.

430 *empty Praise:* praise unaccompanied by material rewards.

John Gay

TRIVIA;
OR, THE ART OF WALKING THE STREETS OF LONDON

Quo te Moeri pedes? An, quo via ducit, in Urbem?[1]

THE pleasure a modern reader of *Trivia* finds in being shown round the unfamiliar streets of eighteenth-century London by an observant and well-informed inhabitant is comparable to, though contrasted with, the pleasure Gay's contemporaries took in its vivid presentation of familiar scenes and incidents from their daily lives. Both kinds of pleasure are legitimate and valuable, but they do not specifically derive from poetry—the *Tatler* and *Spectator* have provided both. *Trivia* offers much more: it is an integrated poetic portrait of city life and human nature as they always have been, so that we are as impressed by the similarities as by the differences between London then and now. The label, "mock-Georgic", which is often attached to the poem, over-emphasises certain aspects at the expense of others, for if there is mockery of the triviality of our daily preoccupations and affairs, there is also an earnest concern with the problems of living in cities; if the classical allusions are sometimes burlesquely inappropriate, they sometimes elevate ordinary events; if London's brutalities and dirt are exposed, its appeal is also experienced and evoked. Night-scenes may be knockabout or lead to meditations on death; the dangers which threaten the unwary pedestrian may be noted with rueful humour or vigorously condemned; comedy and disaster, farce and pathos, satire and eulogy, the sordid and the elegant are all blended in Gay's vision. The medium of this blending is the consciously lofty poetic manner, sometimes underlining mock-heroic ridicule and sometimes dignifying solemn observations and reflections; it is never a pedantic affectation because Gay has such varied uses for it. If not a great poet, he is a very lively and active one: he never marks time, or lacks something interesting to say, and he can always be relied on to say it wittily, humorously, forcefully, or imaginatively in economical, exact and often subtle language.

The text is that of Book III of the first edition of 1714 unchanged.

[1] The epigraph is from Virgil's ninth *Eclogue*, l. 1: "Whither are you walking, Moeris? Are you going, where this road leads, to town?"

OF WALKING THE STREETS BY NIGHT

O Trivia, Goddess, leave these low Abodes,
And traverse o'er the wide Ethereal Roads,
Celestial Queen, put on thy Robes of Light,
Now Cynthia nam'd, fair Regent of the Night.
5 At Sight of thee, the Villain sheaths his Sword,
Nor scales the Wall, to steal the wealthy Hoard.
Oh! may thy Silver Lamp in Heav'n's high Bow'r
Direct my Footsteps in the Midnight Hour.

The Evening.   When Night first bids the twinkling Stars appear,
10   Or with her cloudy Vest inwraps the Air,
Then swarms the busie Street; with Caution tread,
Where the Shop-Windows falling threat thy Head;
Now Lab'rers home return, and join their Strength
To bear the tott'ring Plank, or Ladder's Length;
15   Still fix thy Eyes intent upon the Throng,
And as the Passes open, wind along.

Of the Pass   Where the fair Columns of Saint Clement stand,
of St.   Whose straiten'd Bounds encroach upon the Strand;
Clement's.   Where the low Penthouse bows the Walker's Head,
20   And the rough Pavement wounds the yielding Tread;

1–4 The plural of the Latin word *trivium* ("meeting-place of three roads")
was used generally to mean "the public streets". Trivia was also a name for
the goddess Diana (because she had temples where three roads met), who,
as moon-goddess was usually called Cynthia.

10 *Vest:* robe.

12 *Shop-Windows:* hinged shutters, propped up during the day and let
down at night.

14 *tott'ring:* wobbling, or causing to shake to and fro.

16 *Passes:* bottle-necks in the streets.

17–18 The church of St. Clement Dane's in the Strand was a notorious
obstacle to road-users.

18 *straiten'd Bounds:* confined limits.

19 *Penthouse:* a sloping roof protruding above the window-openings to
protect shops and shoppers from the weather.

Where not a Post protects the narrow Space,
And strung in Twines, Combs dangle in thy Face;
Summon at once thy Courage, rouze thy Care,
Stand firm, look back, be resolute, beware.
25 Forth issuing from steep Lanes, the Collier's Steeds
Drag the black Load; another Cart succeeds,
Team follows Team, Crouds heap'd on Crouds appear,
And wait impatient, 'till the Road grow clear.
Now all the Pavement sounds with trampling Feet,
30 And the mixt Hurry barricades the Street.
Entangled here, the Waggon's lengthen'd Team
Crack the tough Harness; Here a pond'rous Beam
Lies over-turn'd athwart; For Slaughter fed,
Here lowing Bullocks raise their horned Head.
35 Now Oaths grow loud, with Coaches Coaches jar,
And the smart Blow provokes the sturdy War;
From the high Box they whirl the Thong around,
And with the twining Lash their Shins resound:
Their Rage ferments, more dang'rous Wounds they try,
40 And the Blood gushes down their painful Eye.
And now on Foot the frowning Warriors light,
And with their pond'rous Fists renew the Fight;
Blow answers Blow, their Cheeks are 'smear'd with
  Blood,
'Till down they fall, and grappling roll in Mud.
45 So when two Boars, in wild Ytene bred,

21 *not a Post:* Usually in main roads posts separated the footpath from the roadway.

25-6 Between the Strand and the river were many coal-sheds. London's coal had then, of course, to be brought in by sea.

30 *Hurry:* confusion.

31 *lengthen'd:* by the addition of extra horses to pull up the steep streets; or, perhaps, Gay means that the team of horses is stretched out with the strain of pulling the heavy load.

33 *athwart:* across the roadway.   **36** *sturdy:* recklessly violent.

41 *light:* alight.

45 *Ytene:* "New Forest in Hampshire, anciently so call'd." (*Gay, 1714.*) The name was derived from *Iotena*, genitive plural of *Iotan* (Jutes), who occupied the area during the Anglo-Saxon invasion.

Or on Westphalia's fatt'ning Chest-nuts fed,
Gnash their sharp Tusks, and rous'd with equal Fire,
Dispute the Reign of some luxurious Mire;
In the black Flood they wallow o'er and o'er,
50   'Till their arm'd Jaws distill with Foam and Gore.

Of Pick-
Pockets.   Where the Mob gathers, swiftly shoot along,
Nor idly mingle in the noisy Throng.
Lur'd by the Silver Hilt, amid the Swarm,
The subtil Artist will thy Side disarm.
55   Nor is thy Flaxen Wigg with Safety worn;
High on the Shoulder, in the Basket born,
Lurks the sly Boy; whose Hand to Rapine bred,
Plucks off the curling Honours of the Head.
Here dives the skulking Thief, with practis'd Slight,
60   And unfelt Fingers make thy Pocket light.
Where's now thy Watch, with all its Trinkets, flown?
And thy late Snuff-Box is no more thy own.
But lo! his bolder Thefts some Tradesman spies,
Swift from his Prey the scudding Lurcher flies;
65   Dext'rous he scapes the Coach, with nimble Bounds,
While ev'ry honest Tongue *Stop Thief* resounds.
So speeds the wily Fox, alarm'd by Fear,
Who lately filch'd the Turkey's callow Care;
Hounds following Hounds, grow louder as he flies,
70   And injur'd Tenants joyn the Hunter's Cries.
Breathless he stumbling falls: Ill-fated Boy!

46 *Westphalia:* part of Germany, famous for pigs and bacon.
50 *distill with:* drip with.
54 The expert (thief) will steal your sword.
58 *Honours:* wig. See *Windsor-Forest*, p. 52, l. 219 *n.*
59 *Slight:* sleight of hand.
64 *the scudding Lurcher:* the swiftly darting sneak-thief (one who lurks).
65 *Dext'rous he scapes:* He agilely avoids or dodges.
68 *callow Care:* featherless young. (*Callow* comes from Latin *calvus*, "bald".)
70 *injur'd:* who have suffered from the fox's raids.

Why did not honest Work thy Youth employ?
Seiz'd by rough Hands, he's dragg'd amid the Rout,
And stretch'd beneath the Pump's incessant Spout:
75 Or plung'd in miry Ponds, he gasping lies,
Mud choaks his Mouth, and plaisters o'er his Eyes.

Of Ballad-
Singers.   Let not the Ballad-Singer's shrilling Strain
Amid the Swarm thy list'ning Ear Detain:
Guard well thy Pocket; for these Syrens stand,
80 To aid the Labours of the diving Hand;
Confed'rate in the Cheat, they draw the Throng,
And Cambrick Handkerchiefs reward the Song.
But soon as Coach or Cart drives rattling on,
The Rabble part, in Shoals they backward run.
85 So Jove's loud Bolts the mingled War divide,
And Greece and Troy retreats on either side.

Of walking
with a
Friend.   If the rude Throng pour on with furious Pace,
And hap to break thee from a Friend's Embrace,
Stop short; nor struggle thro' the Croud in vain,
90 But watch with careful Eye the passing Train.
Yet I (perhaps too fond) if chance the Tide
Tumultuous, bears my Partner from my Side,
Impatient venture back; despising Harm,
I force my Passage where the thickest swarm.
95 Thus his lost Bride the Trojan sought in vain
Through Night, and Arms, and Flames, and Hills of Slain.
Thus Nisus wander'd o'er the pathless Grove,
To find the brave Companion of his Love,

73 *Rout:* disorderly crowd.
79 *Syrens:* creatures whose singing tempted sailors on to rocks.
82 *Cambrick:* a fine white linen, originally from Cambrai in France.
85–6 In the *Iliad* (Bk. viii) Jove's thunderbolts cause the Greeks to retreat,
not the Trojans.
88 *hap:* chance.   90 *Train:* procession of people.
95–6 Aeneas searched burning Troy for his wife, Creusa.
97–100 Nisus and Euryalus were devoted friends. When, in a night-
attack, they became separated and lost in a forest, Nisus sought for his

The pathless Grove in vain he wanders o'er:
100   Euryalus alas! is now no more.

Of inadver-
tent
Walkers.
      That Walker, who regardless of his Pace,
Turns oft' to pore upon the Damsel's Face,
From Side to Side by thrusting Elbows tost,
Shall strike his aking Breast against the Post;
105   Or Water, dash'd from fishy Stalls, shall stain
His hapless Coat with Spirts of scaly Rain.
But if unwarily he chance to stray,
Where twirling Turnstiles intercept the Way,
The thwarting Passenger shall force them round,
110   And beat the Wretch half breathless to the Ground.

Useful
Precepts.
      Let constant Vigilance thy Footsteps guide,
And wary Circumspection guard thy Side;
Then shalt thou walk unharm'd the dang'rous Night,
Nor need th' officious Link-Boy's smoaky Light.
115   Thou never wilt attempt to cross the Road,
Where Alehouse Benches rest the Porter's Load,
Grievous to heedless Shins; No Barrow's Wheel,
That bruises oft' the Truant School-Boy's Heel,
Behind thee rolling, with insidious Pace,
120   Shall mark thy Stocking with a miry Trace.
Let not thy vent'rous Steps approach too nigh,
Where gaping wide, low steepy Cellars lie;
Should thy Shoe wrench aside, down, down you fall,
And overturn the scolding Huckster's Stall,

friend and tried to rescue him from his captors, but both were killed
(*Aeneid* ix, 381–449).

108 *Turnstiles:* turnstile gates intended to allow only pedestrians to pass.

109 *thwarting:* coming from the other direction.

114 *th' officious Link-Boy's smoaky Light:* Link-boys carried torches and
lit the way for a fee. *Officious* can mean "obliging", but here seems to have
the sense of "pressing his services upon you".

116 *Alehouse Benches:* set up, for the convenience of customers, outside
alehouses.

121–4 Street-traders set up their stalls in open cellars or basements.

125 The scolding Huckster shall not o'er thee moan,
But Pence exact for Nuts and Pears o'erthrown.

Safety first
of all to be
consider'd.

Though you through cleanlier Allies wind by Day,
To shun the Hurries of the publick Way,
Yet ne'er to those dark Paths by Night retire;
130 Mind only Safety, and contemn the Mire.
Then no impervious Courts thy Haste detain,
Nor sneering Ale-Wives bid thee turn again.

The Danger
of crossing
a Square
by Night.

Where Lincoln's-Inn, wide Space, is rail'd around,
Cross not with vent'rous Step; there oft' is found
The lurking Thief, who while the Day-light shone,
Made the Walls eccho with his begging Tone:
That Crutch which late Compassion mov'd, shall wound
Thy bleeding Head, and fell thee to the Ground.
Though thou art tempted by the Link-man's Call,
140 Yet trust him not along the lonely Wall;
In the Mid-way he'll quench the flaming Brand,
And share the Booty with the pilf'ring Band.
Still keep the publick Streets, where oily Rays
Shot from the Crystal Lamp, o'erspread the Ways.

The Happi-
ness of
London.

Happy Augusta! Law-defended Town!
Here no dark Lanthorns shade the Villain's Frown;

130 *contemn:* disregard.

131 *impervious:* with no way out.

132 *Ale-Wives:* women who kept alehouses.

133 *Lincoln's Inn:* Lincoln's Inn Fields. This open space, surrounded by wooden railings, was a notorious haunt of thieves and beggars.

143-4 Oil lamps with thick glass panes illuminated the main streets of London at night. Until the introduction of these lamps in the 1690s, London, like most foreign cities, was lit by lanterns containing candles.

145 *Augusta:* London.

146 *dark Lanthorns:* The "dark-lantern" had a slide which enabled the bearer to conceal the light or let it shine out at one side. It was, thus, a convenience to robbers who could shine it on their victims, without revealing their own faces.

No Spanish Jealousies thy Lanes infest,
Nor Roman Vengeance stabs th' unwary Breast;
Here *Tyranny* ne'er lifts her purple Hand,
150   But Liberty and Justice guard the Land;
No Bravos here profess the bloody Trade,
Nor is the Church the Murd'rer's Refuge made.

Of Chairmen.   Let not the Chairman, with assuming Stride,
Press near the Wall, and rudely thrust thy Side:
155   The Laws have set him Bounds; his servile Feet
Should ne'er encroach where Posts defend the Street.
Yet who the Footman's Arrogance can quell,
Whose Flambeau gilds the Sashes of Pell-mell?
When in long Rank a Train of Torches flame,
160   To light the Midnight Visits of the Dame?
Others, perhaps, by happier Guidance led,
May where the Chairman rests, with Safety tread;
Whene'er I pass, their Poles unseen below,
Make my Knee tremble with the jarring Blow.

Of crossing   If Wheels bar up the Road, where Streets are crost,
the Street.   With gentle Words the Coachman's Ear accost:
He ne'er the Threat, or harsh Command obeys,
But with Contempt the spatter'd Shoe surveys.

147-52 Typical English national pride in the eighteenth century centred on the contrast between the free Englishman, governed by law, and the foreigner, unrestrained in passion but a slave to tyranny.

151 *Bravos:* desperados, assassins.

152 The criminal's right to sanctuary in a church was abolished in England during the seventeenth century.

153 *Chairman:* sedan-chair carrier.

154 *Press near the Wall:* Pedestrians kept, if possible, close to the wall to avoid danger and splashes from passing traffic. Cf. ll. 205-10.

155 *servile:* i.e. belonging to a servant of the public.

158 *Flambeau:* a superior kind of torch, made of waxed wicks, proper to the fashionable quarter.   *Sashes:* windows.   *Pell-mell:* the fashionable pronunciation of Pall-Mall, named after the game once played there.

163 *Poles:* The poles of sedan chairs were fitted low down on the chair.

Now man with utmost Fortitude thy Soul,
170 To cross the Way where Carts and Coaches roll;
Yet do not in thy hardy Skill confide,
Nor rashly risque the Kennel's spacious Stride;
Stay till afar the distant Wheel you hear,
Like dying Thunder in the breaking Air;
175 Thy Foot will slide upon the miry Stone,
And passing Coaches crush thy tortur'd Bone,
Or Wheels enclose the Road; on either Hand
Pent round with Perils, in the midst you stand,
And call for Aid in vain; the Coachman swears,
180 And Carmen drive, unmindful of thy Prayers.
Where wilt thou turn? ah! whither wilt thou fly?
On ev'ry side the pressing Spokes are nigh.
So Sailors, while Charybdis' Gulphs they shun,
Amaz'd, on Scylla's craggy Dangers run.

Of Oysters.   Be sure observe where brown Ostrea stands,
Who boasts her shelly Ware from Wallfleet Sands;
There may'st thou pass, with safe unmiry Feet,
Where the rais'd Pavement leads athwart the Street.
If where Fleet-Ditch with muddy Current flows,
190 You chance to roam; where Oyster-Tubs in Rows

---

172 *Kennel:* wide gutter or drain, often in the middle of the road, which carried away water and refuse.

183-4 A whirlpool and a rock lay on either side of the channel between Italy and Sicily.

185 *Ostrea:* oyster-woman.

186 *Wallfleet Sands:* Even in 1594, Norden reported uncertainty concerning the exact position of Wallfleet. *The Victoria History of the County of Essex* (1907) II, 435, concludes that "as far as one can ascertain, the 'Wallfleet Oysters', which, up to the sixteenth century, were famed above all others, came from the Blackwater estuary". (The fame seems to have lasted well into the eighteenth century.)

189 *Fleet-Ditch:* The Fleet flows from Highgate and Hampstead Ponds, and joins the Thames near Blackfriars Bridge. It was used as an open sewer and frequently choked with mud and refuse. It is now an underground sewer.

Are rang'd beside the Posts; there stay thy Haste,
And with the sav'ry Fish indulge thy Taste:
The Damsel's Knife the gaping Shell commands,
While the salt Liquor streams between her Hands.

195   The Man had sure a Palate cover'd o'er
With Brass or Steel, that on the rocky Shore
First broke the oozy Oyster's pearly Coat,
And risqu'd the living Morsel down his Throat.
What will not Lux'ry taste? Earth, Sea, and Air
200   Are daily ransack'd for the Bill of Fare.
Blood stuff'd in Skins is British Christian's Food,
And France robs Marshes of the croaking Brood;
Spungy Morells in strong Ragousts are found,
And in the Soupe the slimy Snail is drown'd.

Observations concerning keeping the Wall.   When from high Spouts the dashing Torrents fall,
Ever be watchful to maintain the Wall;
For should'st thou quit thy Ground, the rushing Throng
Will with impetuous Fury drive along;
All press to gain those Honours thou hast lost,
210   And rudely shove thee far without the Post.
Then to retrieve the Shed you strive in vain,
Draggled all o'er, and soak'd in Floods of Rain.
Yet rather bear the Show'r, and Toils of Mud,
Than in the doubtful Quarrel risque thy Blood.
215   O think on Œdipus' detested State,
And by his Woes be warn'd to shun thy Fate.

201 *Blood stuff'd in Skins:* black-puddings, made of pig's bladders stuffed with dried blood, suet, etc.
202 *croaking Brood:* frogs.
203 *Morells:* a kind of mushroom.   *Ragousts:* highly-seasoned stews of pieces of meat and vegetables.
206 *maintain the Wall:* keep your position close to the wall. Cf. l. **154** *n.*
210 *without the Post:* outside the posts marking the footway's edge.
211 *Shed:* the shelter of the penthouse roof or overhanging buildings.
212 *Draggled:* wet and dirty.
215–24 Oedipus quarrelled with and killed an old man, whom he met at a cross-roads, not knowing that it was his father, King Laius of Thebes.

    Where three Roads join'd, he met his Sire unknown;
(Unhappy Sire, but more unhappy Son!)
Each claim'd the Way, their Swords the Strife decide,
220 The hoary Monarch fell, he groan'd and dy'd!
Hence sprung the fatal Plague that thinn'd thy Reign,
Thy cursed Incest! and thy Children slain!
Hence wert thou doom'd in endless Night to stray
Through Theban Streets, and cheerless groap thy Way.

Of a Funeral.   Contemplate, Mortal, on thy fleeting Years;
See, with black Train the Funeral Pomp appears!
Whether some Heir attends in sable State,
And mourns with outward Grief a Parent's Fate;
Or the fair Virgin, nipt in Beauty's Bloom,
230 A Croud of Lovers follow to her Tomb.
Why is the Herse with 'Scutcheons blazon'd round,
And with the nodding Plume of Ostrich crown'd?
No: The Dead know it not, nor Profit gain;
It only serves to prove the Living vain.
235 How short is Life! how frail is human Trust!
Is all this Pomp for laying Dust to Dust?

Of avoiding   Where the nail'd Hoop defends the painted Stall,
Paint.   Brush not thy sweeping Skirt too near the Wall;

Having rid Thebes of the Sphinx, he was himself made king and married his mother, Jocasta. Because of this incest, the kingdom was visited with plague. When Oedipus discovered that he was the cause, he blinded himself, and was turned out of his palace to wander through Thebes, and then Greece. His two sons killed each other in battle and his daughter, Antigone, was entombed alive for breaking the edict that her brothers' bodies should not be buried. The story is told in three plays of Sophocles: *Oedipus Rex*, *Oedipus at Colonus*, and *Antigone*.

226 *Pomp:* procession. See *Windsor-Forest*, l. 272 *n*. (But in l. 236 "Pomp" means "ostentatious and splendid ceremony".)

227 *in sable State:* in full black funeral attire.

231–2 Hearses were hung round with coats of arms of the deceased and his family, and surmounted with ostrich plumes.

237 *nail'd Hoop:* fixed to keep passers-by from wet paint.

238 *Skirt:* the hem of a coat.

Thy heedless Sleeve will drink the colour'd Oil
240   And Spot indelible thy Pocket soil.
Has not wise Nature strung the Legs and Feet
With firmest Nerves, design'd to walk the Street?
Has she not given us Hands, to groap aright,
Amidst the frequent Dangers of the Night?
245   And think'st thou not the double Nostril meant,
To warn from oily Woes by previous Scent?

*Of various
Cheats
formerly in
practice.*

Who can the various City Frauds recite,
With all the petty Rapines of the Night?
Who now the Guinea-Dropper's Bait regards,
250   Trick'd by the Sharper's Dice, or Juggler's Cards?
Why shou'd I warn thee ne'er to join the Fray,
Where the Sham-Quarrel interrupts the Way?
Lives there in these our Days so soft a Clown,
Brav'd by the Bully's Oaths, or threat'ning Frown?
255   I need not strict enjoyn the Pocket's Care,
When from the crouded Play thou lead'st the Fair;
Who has not here, or Watch, or Snuff-Box lost,
Or Handkerchiefs that India's Shuttle boast?

*An Admoni-
tion to
Virtue.*

O! may thy Virtue guard thee through the Roads
Of Drury's mazy Courts, and dark Abodes,
The Harlots' guileful Paths, who nightly stand,
Where Katherine-street descends into the Strand.
Say, vagrant Muse, their Wiles and subtil Arts,

242 *Nerves:* sinews.

249 *Guinea-Dropper's Bait:* Guinea-dropping was a kind of confidence trick. A member of the gang would pretend to find a guinea; another would argue about his claim to it; the victim would be called in to settle the matter as a witness. Drinks paid for out of the guinea would be suggested, and the victim then inveigled into card-games, dice, and other ways of losing his money.

254 *Brav'd:* out-faced. (Gay has already spoken of the cowardice of bullies in *Trivia*, i, 59–64.)

258 Indian silk handkerchiefs were expensive.

260 The area round Drury Lane was notorious for its prostitutes.

262 Catherine Street runs parallel to Drury Lane, a little to the west.

To lure the Strangers' unsuspecting Hearts;
265   So shall our Youth on healthful Sinews tread,
And City Cheeks grow warm with rural Red.

How to
know a   'Tis She who nightly strowls with saunt'ring Pace,
Whore.   No stubborn Stays her yielding Shape embrace;
Beneath the Lamp her tawdry Ribbons glare,
270   The new-scower'd Manteau, and the slattern Air;
High-draggled Petticoats her Travels show,
And hollow Cheeks with artful Blushes glow;
With flatt'ring Sounds she sooths the cred'lous Ear,
My noble Captain! Charmer! Love! my Dear!
275   In Riding-hood, near Tavern-Doors she plies,
Or muffled Pinners hide her livid Eyes.
With empty Bandbox she delights to range,
And feigns a distant Errand from the Change;
Nay, she will oft' the Quaker's Hood prophane,
280   And trudge demure the Rounds of Drury-Lane.
She darts from Sarsnet Ambush wily Leers,
Twitches thy Sleeve, or with familiar Airs,
Her Fan will pat thy Cheek; these Snares disdain,
Nor gaze behind thee, when she turns again.

A dreadful   I knew a Ycoman, who for thirst of Gain,
example.   To the great City drove from Devon's Plain

270 *new-scower'd Manteau:* a long, loose, upper gown, newly washed (i.e. second-hand).

271 *High-draggled:* muddy and wet high up from the ankles (showing she has been walking the streets as a lady of fashion would not do).

275 *Riding-hood:* a large hood, shadowing the face.

276 *muffled Pinners:* a head-dress with hanging flaps. By shading the eyes they could conceal the ravages of disease or ill-treatment.   *livid:* leaden-coloured.

277-8 So far Gay has described the prostitute's attempt to pass as a lady of fashion. Now her pretence is to be a shop-girl, carrying a box of millinery from the New Exchange, a building in the Strand, containing many shops.

279 *Quaker's Hood:* The hood worn by female Quakers was regarded as representative of their modesty.

281 *Sarsnet:* a fine silk material often used for lining hoods.

His num'rous lowing Herd; his Herds he sold,
And his deep leathern Pocket bagg'd with Gold;
Drawn by a fraudful Nymph, he gaz'd, he sigh'd;
290 Unmindful of his Home, and distant Bride,
She leads the willing Victim to his Doom,
Through winding Alleys to her Cobweb Room.
Thence thro' the Street he reels, from Post to Post,
Valiant with Wine, nor knows his Treasure lost.
295 The vagrant Wretch th' assembled Watchmen spies,
He waves his Hanger, and their Poles defies;
Deep in the Round-House pent, all Night he snores,
And the next Morn in vain his Fate deplores.

Ah hapless Swain, unus'd to Pains and Ills!
300 Canst thou forgo Roast-Beef for nauseous Pills?
How wilt thou lift to Heav'n thy Eyes and Hands,
When the long Scroll the Surgeon's Fees demands!
Or else (ye Gods avert that worst Disgrace)
Thy ruin'd Nose falls level with thy Face,
305 Then shall thy Wife thy loathsome Kiss disdain,
And wholesome Neighbours from thy Mug refrain.

Of Watch-men. Yet there are Watchmen, who with friendly Light,
Will teach thy reeling Steps to tread aright;
For Sixpence will support thy helpless Arm,
310 And Home conduct thee, safe from nightly Harm;

288 *bagg'd:* sagged, was baggy with. (The *pocket* was a pouch.)

292 *Cobweb Room:* literally suggests a poor and dirty room, but, more importantly, suggests the spider leading the fly into her trap.

296 *Hanger:* short sword. *Poles:* The watchmen whose duty was to prevent crime and disorder in the streets carried long staves.

297 *Round-House:* Round-houses were small lock-ups in which the watchmen detained their prisoners.

300 *forgo Roast-Beef:* The treatment of venereal disease frequently included abstention from "heating" foods.

304 *ruin'd Nose:* a result of venereal disease.

306 *Mug:* They would not wish to use the same drinking-vessels, for instance in the ale-house. (Possibly there is a suggestion that they would keep away from his "ugly face", ruined by disease.)

But if they shake their Lanthorns, from afar,
To call their Breth'ren to confed'rate War,
When Rakes resist their Pow'r; if hapless you
Should chance to wander with the scow'ring Crew;
315 Though Fortune yield thee Captive, ne'er despair,
But seek the Constable's consid'rate Ear;
He will reverse the Watchman's harsh Decree,
Mov'd by the Rhet'rick of a Silver Fee.
Thus would you gain some fav'rite Courtier's Word;
320 Fee not the petty Clarks, but bribe my Lord.

Of Rakes.   Now is the Time that Rakes their Revells keep;
Kindlers of Riot, Enemies of Sleep.
His scatter'd Pence the flying Nicker flings,
And with the Copper Show'r the Casement rings.
325 Who has not heard the Scowrer's Midnight Fame?
Who has not trembled at the Mohock's Name?
Was there a Watchman took his hourly Rounds,
Safe from their Blows, or new-invented Wounds?
I pass their desp'rate Deeds, and Mischiefs done,
330 Where from Snow-hill black steepy Torrents run;

312 *confed'rate War:* a combined attack. Watchmen walked the streets in small groups and signalled to each other with their lanterns. They were under the direction of a constable.

314 *scow'ring Crew:* band of young bullies who attacked people in the streets.

316 *consid'rate Ear:* a play on words: he appears considerate (i.e. shows concern) but awaits a consideration (i.e. a tip or bribe).

318 *Rhet'rick:* persuasion.   **319** *Word:* backing, support.

323 *Nicker:* "Gentlemen, who delighted to break Windows with Halfpence." (*Gay, 1714.*)

323–6 *Nicker . . . Scowrer . . . Mohock:* Three names for the young ruffians, often of good family, who terrorised the streets at night. The *Nicker* rode in coaches and flung coppers to break windows; for *Scowrer,* see l. 314 *n.*; the *Mohocks* were nicknamed after the Mohawk Indians, thought to be particularly savage.

330 Snow Hill is a steep lane which now runs from Holborn Viaduct to Farringdon Street. In the eighteenth century, rainwater from neighbouring districts gathered at Snow-hill ridge and poured down to join the Fleet river at Holborn Bridge.

How Matrons, hoop'd within the Hogshead's Womb,
Were tumbled furious thence, the rolling Tomb
O'er the Stones thunders, bounds from Side to Side.
So Regulus to save his Country dy'd.

A necessary
Caution in
a dark Night.

Where a dim Gleam the paly Lanthorn throws
O'er the mid' Pavement; heapy Rubbish grows,
Or arched Vaults their gaping Jaws extend,
Or the dark Caves to Common-Shores descend.
Oft' by the Winds, extinct the Signal lies,
340   Or smother'd in the glimm'ring Socket dies,
E'er Night has half roll'd round her Ebon Throne;
In the wide Gulph the shatter'd Coach o'erthrown,
Sinks with the snorting Steeds; the Reins are broke,
And from the cracking Axle flies the Spoke.
345   So when fam'd Eddystone's far-shooting Ray,
That led the Sailor through the stormy Way,
Was from its rocky Roots by Billows torn,
And the high Turret in the Whirlewind born,
Fleets bulg'd their Sides against the craggy Land,
350   And pitchy Ruines blacken'd all the Strand.

Who then through Night would hire the harness'd
    Steed,
And who would chuse the rattling Wheel for Speed?

A Fire.   But hark! Distress with screaming Voice draws nigh'r,
And wakes the slumb'ring Street with Cries of Fire.

334 *Regulus:* M. Atilius Regulus, a Roman general, was captured by the
Carthaginians and sent to Rome to advise his countrymen to make peace.
He gave the opposite advice, and, on his return to Carthage was tortured,
and killed by being shut in a chest spiked on the inside with large nails.

338 *Common-Shores:* sewers. (The lanterns were intended to mark where
there were heaps of rubbish in the road, or excavations into vaults or
sewers.)

345 *Eddystone:* Gay is referring to the lighthouse built off Plymouth in
the sixteen-nineties and destroyed by the great storm of 1703.

349 *bulg'd:* struck.

350 *pitchy:* black (but also the seams of ships were sealed with pitch).

355 At first a glowing Red enwraps the Skies,
   And born by Winds the scatt'ring Sparks arise;
   From Beam to Beam, the fierce Contagion spreads;
   The spiry Flames now lift aloft their Heads,
   Through the burst Sash a blazing Deluge pours,
360 And splitting Tiles descend in rattling Show'rs.
   Now with thick Crouds th' enlighten'd Pavement swarms,
   The Fire-man sweats beneath his crooked Arms,
   A leathern Casque his vent'rous Head defends,
   Boldly he climbs where thickest Smoak ascends;
365 Mov'd by the Mother's streaming Eyes and Pray'rs,
   The helpless Infant through the Flame he bears,
   With no less Virtue, than through hostile Fire,
   The Dardan Hero bore his aged Sire.
   See forceful Engines spout their levell'd Streams,
370 To quench the Blaze that runs along the Beams;
   The grappling Hook plucks Rafters from the Walls,
   And Heaps on Heaps the smoaky Ruine falls.
   Blown by strong Winds the fiery Tempest roars,
   Bears down new Walls, and pours along the Floors;
375 The Heav'ns are all a-blaze, the Face of Night
   Is cover'd with a sanguine dreadful Light;
   'Twas such a Light involv'd thy Tow'rs, O Rome,
   The dire Presage of mighty Caesar's Doom,
   When the Sun veil'd in Rust his mourning Head,
380 And frightful Prodigies the Skies o'erspread.
   Hark! the Drum thunders! far, ye Crouds, retire:
   Behold! the ready Match is tipt with Fire,

361 *enlighten'd:* lit by flames.

362 *his crooked Arms:* to protect his face from the heat.

363 *Casque:* helmet.

368 *Dardan:* Dardanus was the mythical ancestor of the Trojans. The *hero* is Aeneas carrying his father, Anchises, out of burning Troy.

369 *forceful Engines:* force-pumps.

378 *dire Presage:* Fires in the sky preceded the murder of Julius Caesar.

381 *the Drum thunders:* A drum was beaten to warn people to keep well away from an explosion. To blow up neighbouring houses was then the most effective way to prevent the spread of a fire.

The nitrous Store is laid, the smutty Train
With running Blaze awakes the barrell'd Grain;
385 Flames sudden wrap the Walls; with sullen Sound,
The shatter'd Pile sinks on the smoaky Ground.
So when the Years shall have revolv'd the Date,
Th' inevitable Hour of Naples' Fate,
Her sap'd Foundations shall with Thunders shake,
390 And heave and toss upon the sulph'rous Lake;
Earth's Womb at once the fiery Flood shall rend,
And in th' Abyss her plunging Tow'rs descend.

Consider, Reader, what Fatigues I've known,
The Toils, the Perils of the wintry Town;
395 What Riots seen, what bustling Crouds I bor'd,
How oft' I cross'd where Carts and Coaches roar'd;
Yet shall I bless my Labours, if Mankind
Their future Safety from my Dangers find.
Thus the bold Traveller, inur'd to Toil,
400 Whose Steps have printed Asia's desert Soil,
The barb'rous Arab's Haunt; or shiv'ring crost
Dark Greenland Mountains of eternal Frost;
Whom Providence, in length of Years, restores
To the wish'd Harbour of his native Shores;
405 Sets forth his Journals to the publick View,
To caution, by his Woes, the wandring Crew.

383 *nitrous Store:* supply of gunpowder.   *smutty Train:* trail of powder.
384 *Grain:* gunpowder.
386 *Pile:* building.
388 Naples, it was thought, must sooner or later be overwhelmed by Vesuvius.
389 *sap'd:* undermined.
390 *the sulph'rous Lake:* The notion is that all the land on which Naples was built would collapse into a subterranean sea of larva smelling of sulphur.
395 *bor'd:* pushed through.
399–406 The early eighteenth century saw the publication of many travel-books, some genuine, some fictitious.
403 *in length of Years:* in course of time.
406 *the wandring Crew:* not his own crew, but all men fond of travel.

> And now compleat my gen'rous Labours lye,
> Finish'd, and ripe for Immortality.
> Death shall entomb in Dust this mould'ring Frame,
410 But never reach th' eternal Part, my Fame.
> When W★ and G★★, mighty Names, are dead;
> Or but at Chelsea under Custards read;
> When Criticks crazy Bandboxes repair,
> And Tragedies, turn'd Rockets, bounce in Air;
415 High-rais'd on Fleetstreet Posts, consign'd to Fame,
> This Work shall shine, and Walkers bless my Name.

409–10 Gay is mock-heroically echoing the lofty claims of many great poets.

411 *W★ and G★★*: Edward Ward and Charles Gildon, two inferior writers often attacked by Pope, Gay and their friends.

412 Chelsea was a pleasure-resort for Londoners, and famous for its buns and cakes. Gay's point is that his poem will last when the works of Ward and Gildon are used to line pie-dishes, when critical writings are used to stiffen collapsing bandboxes, and when tragedies (not being as useful as *Trivia*) are rolled up to make cases for fireworks.

415 *Fleetstreet Posts:* The title-pages of books were nailed, as advertisements, to the doorposts and window-supports of the booksellers (who were, then, also publishers). Fleet Street was a centre of the book-trade.

Thomas Parnell

A NIGHT-PIECE ON DEATH

THERE were many clergymen among eighteenth-century poets, perhaps because the Church seemed the only profession in which a young man of no fortune might advance himself by the exercise of literary gifts. Thomas Parnell (1679–1718) was an Irish cleric, handicapped by fits of depression and heavy drinking, who made little headway in the Church and published few poems during his life-time. He did, however, win the friendship and respect of Swift, Pope, Gay and the other members of the Scriblerus Club, and contributed an "Essay on the Life, Writings and Learning of Homer" to Pope's *Iliad*. After Parnell's death, Pope edited a selection of his friend's work, *Poems on Several Occasions* (1722), which included "A Night-Piece on Death", deservedly the best-known of Parnell's poems, though there are others worthy of more recognition than they have received. Despite some foreshadowings of Gray's *Elegy*, the "Night-Piece" has a distinct character of its own, closer perhaps to "*Il Penseroso*" than to the *Elegy*. Its subdued music has often been admired, but its strength is in the controlled progress from the delicate assonances of the lake-scene, to the crisper and more vigorous discrimination between the three kinds of graves, and finally to the slower, heavier eloquence of Death. "A Hymn for Evening" (which was first published in 1755 in a volume entitled *The Posthumous Works of Dr. Thomas Parnell*) is less varied but has the same assured handling of the octosyllabic couplet, the same unstrained diction and movement, and suggests a more intimate religious emotion than do most of the great eighteenth-century hymns.

The texts are from the first editions, but in the "Night-Piece" I have removed a full-stop at the end of l. 36, and replaced a comma by a full-stop in l. 52.

> By the blue Taper's trembling Light,
> No more I waste the wakeful Night,
> Intent with endless view to pore
> The Schoolmen and the Sages o'er:
> 5 Their Books from Wisdom widely stray,
> Or point at best the longest Way.
> I'll seek a readier Path, and go
> Where Wisdom's surely taught *below*.
>
> How deep yon Azure dies the Sky!
> 10 Where Orbs of Gold unnumber'd lye,
> While thro' their Ranks in silver pride
> The nether Crescent seems to glide.
> The slumb'ring Breeze forgets to breathe,
> The Lake is smooth and clear beneath,
> 15 Where once again the spangled Show
> Descends to meet our Eyes below.
> The Grounds which on the right aspire,
> In dimness from the View retire:

1 *blue:* Candles were said to burn blue as an omen of death, or when spirits were present.

4 *Schoolmen:* men of learning in theology and philosophy.

8 *below:* Normally "here on earth", but here, perhaps, "in the grave".

12 Parnell may mean that the lower side of the moon is lit, or that the moon is lower than the stars through which it "seems to glide".

The Left presents a Place of Graves,
20 Whose Wall the silent Water laves.
That Steeple guides thy doubtful sight
Among the livid gleams of Night.
There pass with melancholy State,
By all the solemn Heaps of Fate,
25 And think, as softly-sad you tread
Above the venerable Dead,
Time was, like thee they Life possest,
And Time shall be, that thou shalt Rest.

Those Graves, with bending Osier bound,
30 That nameless heave the crumbled Ground,
Quick to the glancing Thought disclose
Where *Toil* and *Poverty* repose.

The flat smooth Stones that bear a Name,
The Chissel's slender help to Fame,
35 (Which e'er our Sett of Friends decay
Their frequent Steps may wear away)
A *middle Race* of Mortals own,
Men, half ambitious, all unknown.

The Marble Tombs that rise on high,
40 Whose Dead in vaulted Arches lye,
Whose Pillars swell with sculptur'd Stones,
Arms, Angels, Epitaphs, and Bones,
These (all the poor Remains of State)
Adorn the *Rich*, or praise the *Great*;
45 Who while on Earth in Fame they live,
Are sensless of the Fame they give.

Ha! while I gaze, pale Cynthia fades,

22 *livid:* "of a bluish leaden colour" (O.E.D.).
23 *State:* "dignity of demeanour" (O.E.D.).
43 *State:* "high rank, greatness, power" (O.E.D.).
47 *Cynthia:* moon-goddess. The moonlight is dimmed by the shadowy
vision.

The bursting Earth unveils the Shades!
All slow, and wan, and wrap'd with Shrouds,
50   They rise in visionary Crouds,
And all with sober Accent cry,
Think, Mortal, what it is to dye.

Now from yon black and fun'ral Yew,
That bathes the Charnel House with Dew,
55   Methinks I hear a *Voice* begin;
(Ye Ravens, cease your croaking Din,
Ye tolling Clocks, no Time resound
O'er the long Lake and midnight Ground)
It sends a Peal of hollow Groans,
60   Thus speaking from among the Bones.

When Men my Scythe and Darts supply,
How great a *King* of *Fears* am I!
They view me like the last of Things:
They make, and then they dread, my Stings.
65   Fools! if you less provok'd your Fears,
No more my Spectre-Form appears.
Death's but a Path that must be trod,
If Man wou'd ever pass to God:
A Port of Calms, a State of Ease
70   From the rough Rage of swelling Seas.

Why then thy flowing sable Stoles,
Deep pendent Cypress, mourning Poles,

48 *Shades:* spirits of the dead.
50 *visionary:* seen as though in a vision.
54 *Charnel House:* vault, place where disinterred bones were kept.
61 The imagination of men furnishes Death with his fearful weapons.
65 *provok'd:* summoned.
71–6 These lines describe traditional funeral paraphernalia. *Stoles* were long, mourning robes; *Cypress* was a light material used in mourning drapings and attire, although the reference might possibly be to the cypress tree, branches of which were hung up at funerals to symbolise mourning. *Scarves* of black silk or crape were worn at funerals. Long *Poles* were carried by the attendants who stood round the coffin or followed it in the procession. *Herses* were originally stationary structures to support the *Palls*

Loose Scarfs to fall athwart thy Weeds,
Long Palls, drawn Herses, cover'd Steeds,
75 And Plumes of black, that as they tread,
Nod o'er the 'Scutcheons of the Dead?

Nor can the parted Body know,
Nor wants the Soul, these Forms of Woe:
As Men who long in Prison dwell,
80 With Lamps that glimmer round the Cell,
When e'er their suffering Years are run,
Spring forth to greet the glitt'ring Sun:
Such Joy, tho' far transcending Sense,
Have pious Souls at parting hence.
85 On Earth, and in the Body plac't,
A few, and evil Years, they wast:
But when their Chains are cast aside,
See the glad Scene unfolding wide,
Clap the glad Wing and tow'r away,
90 And mingle with the Blaze of Day.

("long draperies") above the coffin: *drawn* (i.e. horse-drawn) hearses
developed in the mid-seventeenth century. The horses were hung with
black cloths reaching almost to the ground, and the hearse was surmounted
with ostrich plumes and adorned with banners bearing the coats-of-arms of
the deceased and his family. See *Trivia*, p. 73, ll. 231-2.

77 *parted:* departed.
89 *tow'r away:* soar aloft (an expression from hawking).

A HYMN FOR EVENING

The beam-repelling mists arise,
And ev'ning spreads obscurer skies:
The twilight will the night forerun,
And night itself be soon begun.
5 Upon thy knees devoutly bow
And pray the Lord of glory now,
To fill thy breast, or deadly sin
May cause a blinder night within.

And whether pleasing vapours rise,
10 Which gently dim the closing eyes,
Which makes the weary members bless'd,
With sweet refreshment in their rest;
Or whether spirits in the brain,
Dispel their soft embrace again,
15 And on my watchful bed I stay,
Forsook by sleep and waiting day;
Be God for ever in my view
And never he forsake me too;
But still as day concludes in night,
20 To break again with new born light,
His wond'rous bounty let me find
With still a more enlighten'd mind,
When grace and love in one agree,
Grace from God, and love from me,
25 Grace that will from heav'n inspire,
Love that seals it in desire,
Grace and love that mingle beams,
And fill me with encreasing flames.
Thou that hast thy palace far
30 Above the moon and ev'ry star,
Thou that sittest on a throne,
To which the night was never known,
Regard my voice and make me bless'd,
By kindly granting its request.
35 If thoughts on thee my soul employ,
My darkness will afford me joy.
'Till thou shalt call, and I shall soar,
And part with darkness evermore.

15 *watchful:* wakeful.

19 *still:* always.

25–6 Heavenly grace will inspire the union, and man's love for God brings the desire for such a compact which seals it.

John Dyer

GRONGAR HILL

JOHN DYER (1699–1757) was born and grew up near Grongar Hill, which overlooks the valley of the Towy in Carmarthenshire, and his familiar affection for the scene is manifest in both the poems he wrote there in 1726. He had returned from two years in Italy (where he had been studying to become a painter) to stay with his brother at Aberglasney at the foot of the hill. Grongar Hill became as famous as Cooper's Hill. Echoes of Dyer's poem occur throughout the eighteenth century, for Dyer was particularly fortunate in the response of other poets to his work. James Thomson and Richard Savage admired it; Mark Akenside said that he would be prepared to judge an age's claim to taste in poetry by its appreciation of Dyer's poem, *The Fleece*, and Wordsworth wrote a sonnet "To the poet, John Dyer" which concluded that, despite neglect,

> Yet pure and powerful minds, hearts meek and still,
> A grateful few, shall love thy modest lay . . .
> Long as the thrush shall pipe on Grongar Hill!

Compared with earlier prospects, Dyer's is more colourful and intimate; instead of political messages, he found homely moral truths in the landscape, much more suited to the mood of the century.

The text of "A Country Walk" is from *Miscellaneous Poems and Translations*, edited by Richard Savage in 1726 (except that I have corrected the spelling of Aberglasney (l. 153) which was misspelt "Abergasney"). The same volume included a pindaric ode entitled "Grongar Hill" (presumably the earliest form), but later, in the same year, an octosyllabic version appeared in *A New Miscellany*. This was, however, rather unpolished, and the form in which the poem attained popularity was first published in D. Lewis's *Miscellaneous Poems by Several Hands* (also dated 1726). This is the text printed below, although I have inserted from later editions line 147, apparently omitted inadvertently.

Silent Nymph, with curious Eye!
Who, the purple Ev'ning, lye
On the Mountain's lonely Van,
Beyond the Noise of busy Man,
5   Painting fair the form of Things,
While the yellow Linnet sings;
Or the tuneful Nightingale
Charms the Forest with her Tale;
Come with all thy various Hues,
10 Come, and aid thy Sister Muse;
Now while Phœbus riding high
Gives Lustre to the Land and Sky!
Grongar Hill invites my Song,
Draw the Landskip bright and strong;
15 Grongar, in whose Mossie Cells
Sweetly-musing Quiet dwells:
Grongar, in whose silent Shade,
For the modest Muses made,
So oft I have, the Even still,

1 *Silent Nymph:* The Pindaric version of the poem begins:

> *Fancy!* Nymph that loves to lie
> On the lonely Eminence.

But here the poet-painter Dyer may be calling on the non-vocal Sister-Muse of Painting to assist his poetic Muse. Such words as "Painting", "Hues", and "Draw" seem to confirm that he wants to use his painter's eye in his poetic composition.

2 *lye:* Dyer's grammar was roughly handled in *Notes and Queries* (1871). One correspondent suggested that "dost" should be read or inserted after "who".

3 *Van:* front, i.e. side facing the valley.

6 *yellow Linnet:* It has been objected that there is no yellow linnet. But according to the Rev. C. Swainson (*The Folk Lore and Provincial Names of British Birds*, 1886) "linnet" was in Shropshire a local name for the goldfinch, and it is possible that Dyer became acquainted with it during his journeys around Wales and the neighbouring counties.

11 *Phœbus:* Another name for Apollo, the sun-god.

14 *Landskip:* landscape.   15 *Cells:* caves.

19 *the Even still:* in the quiet evening.

20 At the Fountain of a Rill,
    Sate upon a flow'ry Bed,
    With my Hand beneath my Head;
    And stray'd my Eyes o'er Towy's Flood,
    Over Mead, and over Wood,
25 From House to House, from Hill to Hill,
    'Till Contemplation had her fill.
        About his chequer'd Sides I wind,
    And leave his Brooks and Meads behind,
    And Groves, and Grottoes where I lay,
30 And Vistoes shooting Beams of Day:
    Wider and wider spreads the Vale;
    As Circles on a smooth Canal:
    The Mountains round, unhappy Fate,
    Sooner or later, of all Height!
35 Withdraw their Summits from the Skies,
    And lessen as the others rise:
    Still the Prospect wider spreads,
    Adds a thousand Woods and Meads,
    Still it widens, widens still,
40 And sinks the newly-risen Hill.
        Now, I gain the Mountain's Brow,
    What a Landskip lies below!
    No Clouds, no Vapours intervene,
    But the gay, the open Scene
45 Does the Face of Nature show,
    In all the Hues of Heaven's Bow!

27 *chequer'd:* variegated.

29 *Grottoes:* caves; but these are probably artificially improved for the convenience of walkers on the estate.

30 *Vistoes:* an alternative spelling of "vistas". Dyer is, perhaps, thinking of sunbeams shining into a wood through openings designed to afford striking views.

32 *Canal:* an artificial pond or lake.

34–40 As he ascends, the surrounding hills appear to be diminished. He can see higher ones behind them, but these, in turn, having risen into view, seem to become smaller as he mounts the hill.

And, swelling to embrace the Light,
Spreads around beyond the Sight.
  Old Castles on the Cliffs arise,
50 Proudly tow'ring in the Skies!
Rushing from the Woods, the Spires
Seem from hence ascending Fires!
Half his Beams Apollo sheds,
On the yellow Mountain-Heads!
55 Gilds the Fleeces of the Flocks;
And glitters on the broken Rocks!
  Below me Trees unnumber'd rise,
Beautiful in various Dies:
The gloomy Pine, the Poplar blue,
60 The yellow Beech, the sable Yew,
The slender Firr, that taper grows,
The sturdy Oak with broad-spread Boughs.
And beyond the purple Grove,
Haunt of Phillis, queen of Love!
65 Gawdy as the op'ning Dawn,
Lies a long and level Lawn,
On which a dark Hill, steep and high,
Holds and charms the wand'ring Eye!
Deep are his Feet in Towy's Flood,
70 His Sides are cloath'd with waving Wood,
And antient Towers crown his Brow,
That cast an awful Look below;
Whose ragged Walls the Ivy creeps,
And with her Arms from falling Keeps;
75 So both a Safety from the Wind
On mutual Dependance find.

49 *Old Castles:* Among the ruined castles visible from Grongar Hill are Carreg Cennen Castle, Dynevor Castle and Dryslwyn Castle.

63–64 Golden Grove is visible from Grongar. *Purple* here means merely "richly coloured". The name *Phillis* is probably taken from Virgil's *Eclogues* where it belongs to a beautiful country-girl. In *Eclogues* VIII she is associated with a list of trees.

66 ff. There has been some disagreement as to which ruin Dyer was looking at—Dynevor Castle or Dryslwyn Castle.

'Tis now the Raven's bleak Abode;
'Tis now th' Apartment of the Toad;
And there the Fox securely feeds;
80   And there the pois'nous Adder breeds,
Conceal'd in Ruins, Moss and Weeds:
While, ever and anon, there falls,
Huge heaps of hoary moulder'd Walls.
Yet Time has seen, that lifts the low,
85   And level lays the lofty Brow,
Has seen this broken Pile compleat,
Big with the Vanity of State;
But transient is the Smile of Fate!
A little Rule, a little Sway,
90   A Sun-beam in a Winter's Day
Is all the Proud and Mighty have,
Between the Cradle and the Grave.
    And see the Rivers how they run,
Thro' Woods and Meads, in Shade and Sun,
95   Sometimes swift, and sometimes slow,
Wave succeeding Wave they go
A various Journey to the Deep,
Like human Life to endless Sleep!
Thus is Nature's Vesture wrought,
100   To instruct our wand'ring Thought;
Thus she dresses green and gay,
To disperse our Cares away.
    Ever charming, ever new,
When will the Landskip tire the View!
105   The Fountain's Fall, the River's Flow,
The woody Vallies, warm and low;
The windy Summit, wild and high,
Roughly rushing on the Sky!
The pleasent Seat, the ruin'd Tow'r,
110   The naked Rock, the shady Bow'r;
The Town and Village, Dome and Farm,
Each give each a double Charm,
As Pearls upon an Æthiop's Arm.

86 *Pile:* building.   **111** *Dome:* a large house.

     See on the Mountain's southern side, ⎫
115 Where the Prospect opens wide,   ⎬
     Where the Ev'ning gilds the Tide; ⎭
     How close and small the Hedges lie!
     What streaks of Meadows cross the Eye!
     A Step methinks may pass the Stream,
120 So little distant Dangers seem;
     So we mistake the Future's face,
     Ey'd thro' Hope's deluding Glass;
     As yon Summits soft and fair,
     Clad in Colours of the Air,
125 Which, to those who journey near,
     Barren, and brown, and rough appear;
     Still we tread tir'd the same coarse Way.
     The Present's still a cloudy Day.
     O may I with my self agree,
130 And never covet what I see:
     Content me with an humble Shade,
     My Passions tam'd, my Wishes laid;
     For while our Wishes wildly roll,
     We banish Quiet from the Soul:
135 'Tis thus the Busy beat the Air;
     And Misers gather Wealth and Care.
     Now, ev'n now, my Joy runs high,
     As on the Mountain-turf I lie;
     While the wanton Zephir sings,
140 And in the Vale perfumes his Wings;
     While the Waters murmur deep;
     While the Shepherd charms his Sheep;
     While the Birds unbounded fly, ⎫
     And with Musick fill the Sky. ⎬
145 Now, ev'n now, my Joy runs high. ⎭
     Be full, ye Courts, be great who will;
     Search for Peace with all your Skill:
     Open wide the lofty Door,
     Seek her on the marble Floor,

116 *Tide:* river.   **131** *Shade:* place of shelter.
139 *wanton Zephir:* playful breeze (strictly, west wind).

150 In vain ye search, she is not there;
  In vain ye search the Domes of Care!
  Grass and Flowers Quiet treads,
  On the Meads, and Mountain-heads,
  Along with Pleasure, close ally'd,
155 Ever by each other's Side:
  And often, by the murm'ring Rill, }
  Hears the Thrush, while all is still,
  Within the Groves of Grongar Hill.

A COUNTRY WALK

The Morning's fair, the lusty Sun,
With ruddy Cheek begins to run;
And early Birds, that wing the Skies,
Sweetly sing to see him rise.

5   I am resolv'd, this charming Day,
  In the open Field to stray,
  And have no Roof above my Head,
  But that whereon the Gods do tread.
  Before the yellow Barn I see
10 A beautiful Variety
  Of strutting Cocks, advancing stout,
  And flirting empty Chaff about.
  Hens, Ducks, and Geese, and all their Brood,
  And Turkeys gobling for their Food;
15 While Rusticks thrash the wealthy Floor,
  And tempt all to crowd the Door.

  What a fair Face does Nature show?
  Augusta, wipe thy dusty Brow;
  A Landskip wide salutes my Sight,
20 Of shady Vales, and Mountains bright;

16 "Them" is often supplied after "tempt", but the metre does not absolutely require it.

18 *Augusta*: London, as a typical city. (Cf. *Windsor-Forest*, p. 58, l. 334.)

And azure Heavens I behold,
And Clouds of Silver and of Gold.
And now into the Fields I go,
Where Thousand flaming Flowers glow;
25   And every neighb'ring Hedge I greet,
With Honey-suckles smelling sweet.
Now o'er the daisy Meads I stray,
And meet with, as I pace my way,
Sweetly shining on the Eye,
30   A Riv'let gliding smoothly by;
Which shews with what an easy Tide
The Moments of the happy glide.
Here, finding Pleasure after Pain,
Sleeping I see a wearied Swain,
35   While his full Scrip lies open by,
That does his healthy Food supply.

Happy Swain, sure happier far
Than lofty Kings and Princes are!
Enjoy sweet Sleep, which shuns the Crown,
40   With all its easy Beds of Down.

The Sun now shows his Noon-tide Blaze,
And sheds around me burning Rays.
A little onward, and I go
Into the Shade that Groves bestow;
45   And on green Moss I lay me down,
That o'er the Root of Oak has grown;
Where all is silent, but some Flood,
That sweetly murmurs in the Wood;
But Birds that warble in the Sprays,
50   And charm ev'n *Silence* with their Lays.

Oh pow'rful *Silence*, how you reign
In the Poet's busy Brain!
His num'rous Thoughts obey the Calls
Of the tuneful Water-falls.

35 *Scrip:* small bag or satchel.

55 Like Moles, whene'er the Coast is clear, ⎫
    They rise before thee without Fear,   ⎬
    And range in Parties here and there.   ⎭

    Some wildly to Parnassus wing,
    And view the fair Castalian Spring;
60 Where they behold a lonely Well,
    Where now no tuneful Muses dwell;
    But now and then a slavish Hind
    Padling the troubled Pool they find.

    Some trace the pleasing Paths of Joy,
65 Others the blissful Scene destroy;
    In thorny Tracks of Sorrow stray,
    And pine for Clio far away.
    But stay—Methinks her Lays I hear,
    So smooth! so sweet! so deep! so clear!
70 No, 'tis not her Voice I find,
    'Tis but the *Eccho* stays behind.

    Some meditate ambitious Brow,
    And the black Gulph that gapes below:
    Some peep in Courts, and there they see
75 The sneaking Tribe of Flattery.
    But, striking to the Ear and Eye,
    A nimble Deer comes bounding by!
    When rushing from yon rustling Spray,
    It made 'em vanish all away.

59 *Castalian Spring:* a spring on Mount Parnassus, sacred to Apollo, God of Poetry, and the Muses. Cf. *Cooper's Hill*, p. 24, l. 2.

60–3 Greece was under Turkish rules; but Dyer may be criticising contemporary poets.

67 *Clio:* one of the pen-names of the poetess, Martha Fowke Sansom, who had some verses in this collection.

69 Cf. *Cooper's Hill*, p. 32, l. 191.

72–3 Dyer is using landscape terms to describe his thoughts. The "Brow" is a high crag with a deep drop beneath, emblematic of ambition. Cf. *The Task*, p. 162, ll. 57 ff.

80   I rouse me up, and on I rove,
'Tis more than time to leave the Grove.
The Sun declines, the Evening Breeze
Begins to whisper thro' the Trees;
And as I leave the Sylvan Gloom,
85   As to the Glare of Day I come,
An old Man's smoky Nest I see,
Leaning on an aged Tree;
Whose willow Walls and furzy Brow
A little Garden sway below.

90   Thro' spreading Beds of blooming Green,
Matted with Herbage sweet, and clean,
A Vein of Water limps along,
And makes 'em ever green, and young.
Here he puffs upon his Spade,
95   And digs up Cabbage in the Shade:
His tatter'd Rags are sable brown,
His Beard and Hair are hoary grown;
The dying Sap descends apace,
And leaves a wither'd Hand and Face.

100   Up Grongar hill I labour now,
And catch at last his Bushy Brow.
Oh how fresh, how pure the Air!
Let me breathe a little here.
Where am I, Nature? I descry
105   Thy Magazine before me lie!
Temples!—and Towns!—and Tow'rs!—and Woods!
And Hills!—and Vales!—and Fields!—and Floods!
Crowding before me, edg'd around
With naked Wilds, and barren Ground.

110   See below the pleasant Dome,
The Poet's pride, the Poet's Home,
Which the Sun-Beams shine upon,
To the Even, from the Dawn.

100 *Grongar hill:* "A Hill in South Wales." (*Dyer, 1726.*)
103 *breathe:* take my breath.   **105** *Magazine:* varied store.
110 *Dome:* house.

See her Woods where *Eccho* talks,
115   Her Gardens trim, her Terras Walks,
Her Wildernesses, fragrant Brakes,
Her gloomy Bowers, and shining Lakes.
Keep, ye Gods, this humble Seat,
For ever pleasant, private, neat.

120   See yonder Hill, uprising steep,
Above the River slow and deep:
It looks from hence a Pyramid,
Beneath a verdant Forest hid;
On whose high Top there rises great,
125   The mighty Remnant of a Seat,
An old green Tow'r, whose batter'd Brow
Frowns upon the Vale below.

    Look upon that flow'ry Plain,
How the Sheep surround their Swain,   ⎫
130   How they crowd to hear his Strain!   ⎬
All careless, with his Legs across,   ⎭
Leaning on a Bank of Moss,
He spends his empty Hours at play,
Which fly as light as Down away.

135   And there behold a bloomy Mead,
A Silver Stream, a Willow Shade,
Beneath the Shade a Fisher stand,
Who, with the Angle in his Hand,
Swings the nibling Fry to Land.

140   In Blushes the descending Sun,
Kisses the Streams, while slow they run;
And yonder Hill remoter grows,
Or dusky Clouds do interpose.
The Fields are left, the lab'ring Hind
145   His weary Oxen does unbind;

116 *Wildernesses:* parts of a garden, planted with trees to provide winding walks.   **120** *yonder Hill:* Cf. "Grongar Hill", p. 90, ll. 67 ff.

And vocal Mountains, as they low,
Re-eccho to the Vales below.
The jocund Shepherds piping come,
And drive the Herd before 'em home;
150   And now begin to light their Fires,
Which send up Smoke in curling Spires!
While, with light Hearts, All homeward tend,
To Aberglasney I descend.

But, Oh! how bless'd wou'd be the Day, ⎫
155   Did I with Clio pace my way,   ⎬
And not alone, and solitary stray.   ⎭

153 *Aberglasney:* "The Name of a Seat belonging to the Author's Brother." (*Dyer, 1726.*)

James Thomson

from THE SEASONS

DESPITE Dr. Johnson's complaint that *The Seasons* lack "method", each of the four sections is methodically and appropriately ordered. It is proper that *Spring* should trace the rebirth of life and love in the whole creation, proceeding "from the lower to the higher"; that *Summer*, which is the least developing of the seasons, should be confined to a single day; that *Autumn* should centre round harvest from the ripening of the crops to the celebrations after the gathering in; and that *Winter* should sink from cold weather, to storms, snow, and bitter frost, until in the depths of the season, new hope springs in the vision of a resurrection:

The Storms of wintry Time will quickly pass
And one unbounded Spring encircle all.

But it is not only because of the grand general design that *The Seasons* needs to be read in its entirety. Many critics, who have praised Thomson's descriptive powers, have belittled or ridiculed the passages of moral, philosophical, theological, and political reflection and declamation. Separate the poem in this way, and it is easy to mock at the poet's celebration of the divine benevolence, as though it were shallow optimism, or, on the other hand, to regard him as "merely" a descriptive poet. In fact, Thomson's vision is moving, precisely because it holds in tension the faith that the ways of God, though mysterious, are manifestations of love for man, and the knowledge of a universe whose awe-inspiring powers brush aside man, his works, and his purposes. The "thought" of the poem cannot be detached from the descriptions and discarded: it runs throughout, as much in the storms and torrents and snowstorms as in the explicitly didactic passages.

It is damaging, then, to represent Thomson by extracts, however long. Yet, although he cannot be omitted from a collection of poetry where he is perhaps the greatest single influence, one cannot include the 5,541 lines of *The Seasons* nor even the shortest section, *Winter*. It is true that when *Winter* first appeared in 1726, it consisted of only 405 lines, but after Thomson's final revision, although nearly a hundred lines of the original version had been transferred to *Autumn*, the section had grown to 1,069 lines. It was, in fact, a substantially new poem, and in the following extracts I have used, not the 1730 *Autumn* and 1726 *Winter*, but the final edition of the whole poem prepared by the author, which appeared in 1746 and has been the basis of all subsequent editions.

In fairness to Dr. Johnson, with whom I began by disagreeing, it should be said that his general summing-up of Thomson has not been improved on:

He thinks in a peculiar train, and he thinks always as a man of genius; he looks round on Nature and on Life with the eye which Nature bestows only on a poet, the eye that distinguishes in every thing presented to its view whatever there is on which imagination can delight to be detained, and with a mind that at once comprehends the vast, and attends to the minute. The reader of *The Seasons* wonders that he never saw before what Thomson shews him, and that he never yet has felt what Thomson impresses.

from AUTUMN (lines 1093–1175)

    The Western Sun withdraws the shorten'd Day;
And humid Evening, gliding o'er the Sky,
In her chill Progress, to the Ground condens'd
The Vapours throws. Where creeping Waters ooze,
5 Where Marshes stagnate, and where Rivers wind,
Cluster the rolling Fogs, and swim along
The dusky-mantled Lawn. Mean-while the Moon
Full-orb'd, and breaking thro the scatter'd Clouds,

7 *The dusky-mantled Lawn:* the glade wrapped in gathering darkness.

Shews her broad Visage in the crimson'd East.
10   Turn'd to the Sun direct, her spotted Disk,
Where Mountains rise, umbrageous Dales descend,
And Caverns deep, as optic Tube descries,
A smaller Earth, gives all his Blaze again,
Void of its Flame, and sheds a softer Day.
15   Now thro the passing Cloud she seems to stoop,
Now up the pure Cerulean rides sublime.
Wide the pale Deluge floats, and streaming mild
O'er the sky'd Mountain to the shadowy Vale,
While Rocks and Floods reflect the quivering Gleam,
20   The whole Air whitens with a boundless Tide
Of silver Radiance, trembling round the World.

But when half-blotted from the Sky her Light,
Fainting, permits the starry Fires to burn,
With keener Luster thro the Depth of Heaven;
25   Or quite extinct her deaden'd Orb appears,
And scarce appears, of sickly beamless White;
Oft in this Season, silent from the North
A Blaze of Meteors shoots: ensweeping first
The lower Skies, they all at once converge
30   High to the Crown of Heaven, and all at once
Relapsing quick as quickly reascend,

9 In autumn, farmers speak of a "harvest moon" when moonrise coincides with sunset, thus enabling harvesters to work later.

11-12 The irregularities of the moon's surface, as seen through a telescope, are described in terms of the earth's surface. Cf. the terms "Sea" and "Mountain" still used of lunar features.

14 *Flame:* heat.

15 *stoop:* swoop down (a term from hawking).

16 *Cerulean:* blue sky.

17 *the pale Deluge:* moonlight.

18 *sky'd:* lofty, reaching to the skies.

28 *A Blaze of Meteors:* The Aurora Borealis was thought to be produced by meteors. There had been a famous and spectacular Aurora on March 6, 1716, which led to many published discussions of the cause and significance of these phenomena.

And mix, and thwart, extinguish, and renew,
All Ether coursing in a Maze of Light.

From Look to Look, contagious thro the Croud,
35   The Pannic runs, and into wondrous Shapes
Th' Appearance throws: Armies in meet Array,
Throng'd with aërial Spears, and Steeds of Fire;
Till the long Lines of full-extended War
In bleeding Fight commixt, the sanguine Flood
40   Rolls a broad Slaughter o'er the Plains of Heaven.
As thus they scan the visionary Scene,
On all sides swells the superstitious Din,
Incontinent; and busy Frenzy talks
Of Blood and Battle; Cities over-turn'd,
45   And late at night in swallowing Earthquake sunk,
Or hideous wrapt in fierce ascending Flame;
Of sallow Famine, Inundation, Storm;
Of Pestilence, and every great Distress;
Empires subvers'd, when ruling Fate has struck
50   Th' unalterable Hour: even Nature's self
Is deem'd to totter on the Brink of Time.
Not so the Man of philosophic Eye,
And Inspect sage; the waving Brightness he
Curious surveys, inquisitive to know
55   The Causes, and Materials, yet unfix'd,
Of this Appearance beautiful, and new.

Now black, and deep, the Night begins to fall,
A Shade immense. Sunk in the quenching Gloom,
Magnificent and vast, are Heaven and Earth.
60   Order confounded lies; all Beauty void;

33 *Ether:* the medium which was thought to fill space; hence, the sky.
35–6 Fear makes people see strange visions in the Aurora Borealis.
36 *meet:* fitting (i.e. for armies of the sky).
49 *subvers'd:* overturn'd.
52 *philosophic:* scientific. (What we would now call "science" was in the eighteenth century called "natural philosophy".)
53 *Inspect:* examination.

Distinction lost; and gay Variety
One universal Blot: such the fair Power
Of Light, to kindle and create the Whole.
Drear is the State of the benighted Wretch,
65   Who then, bewilder'd, wanders thro the Dark,
Full of pale Fancies, and Chimeras huge;
Nor visited by one directive Ray,
From Cottage streaming, or from airy Hall.
Perhaps impatient as he stumbles on,
70   Struck from the Root of slimy Rushes, blue,
The Wild fire scatters round, or gather'd trails
A Length of Flame deceitful o'er the Moss;
Whither decoy'd by the fantastick Blaze,
Now lost and now renew'd, he sinks absorpt,
75   Rider and Horse, amid the miry Gulf:
While still, from Day to Day, his pining Wife,
And plaintive Children his Return await,
In wild Conjecture lost. At other Times,
Sent by the *better Genius* of the Night,
80   Innoxious, gleaming on the Horse's Mane,
The Meteor sits; and shews the narrow Path,
That winding leads thro Pits of Death, or else
Instructs him how to take the dangerous Ford.

66 *Chimeras:* wild and grotesque imaginings.

71 *Wild fire: ignis fatuus,* will o' the wisp, jack o' lantern: a flickering light produced by marsh-gas.

74 *absorpt:* swallowed up.

79 *better Genius:* Thomson imagines the night possessed of two spirits— an evil genius which sends the misleading lights and a benevolent genius which sends the helpful lights.

80 *Innoxious:* harmless.

81 *Meteor: ignis lambens* (a faint electrical light, like St. Elmo's fire or corposant usually seen on the extremities of ships' masts).

II

from WINTER (lines 41–322)

Now when the chearless Empire of the Sky
To Capricorn the Centaur-Archer yields,
And fierce Aquarius, stains th' inverted Year;
Hung o'er the farthest Verge of Heaven, the Sun
5 Scarce spreads o'er Ether the dejected Day.
Faint are his Gleams, and ineffectual shoot
His struggling Rays, in horizontal Lines,
Thro the thick Air; as cloath'd in cloudy Storm,
Weak, wan, and broad, he skirts the Southern Sky;
10 And, soon-descending, to the long dark Night,
Wide-shading All, the prostrate World resigns.
Nor is the Night unwish'd; while vital Heat,
Light, Life, and Joy, the dubious Day forsake.
Mean-time, in sable Cincture, Shadows vast,
15 Deep-ting'd and damp, and congregated Clouds,
And all the vapoury Turbulence of Heaven
Involve the Face of Things. Thus Winter falls,
A heavy Gloom oppressive o'er the World,
Thro Nature shedding Influence malign,
20 And rouses up the Seeds of dark Disease.
The Soul of Man dies in him, loathing Life,
And black with more than melancholy Views.
The Cattle droop; and o'er the furrow'd Land,
Fresh from the Plow, the dun discolour'd Flocks,
25 Untended spreading, crop the wholesome Root.
Along the Woods, along the moorish Fens,

1–3 The sun passes from the zodiacal sign of Sagittarius (the Archer) into that of Capricorn (the Goat) in late December, and from thence into the sign of Aquarius (the water-carrier) in late January.

3 *stains th' inverted Year:* darkens the wintry days. (The year is "inverted" because the sun has apparently passed south of the equator.)

5 *dejected:* cast down. (Here the word suggests both "low-spirited" and "low in the sky".)

14 *sable Cincture:* encircling blackness.   **24** *dun:* dark.

Sighs the sad *Genius* of the coming Storm;
And up among the loose disjointed Cliffs,
And fractur'd Mountains wild, the brawling Brook
30   And Cave, presageful, send a hollow Moan,
Resounding long in listening Fancy's Ear.

Then comes the Father of the Tempest forth,
Wrapt in black Glooms. First joyless Rains obscure
Drive thro the mingling Skies with Vapour foul;
35   Dash on the Mountain's Brow, and shake the Woods,
That grumbling wave below. Th' unsightly Plain
Lies a brown Deluge; as the low-bent Clouds
Pour Flood on Flood, yet unexhausted still
Combine, and deepening into Night shut up
40   The Day's fair Face. The Wanderers of Heaven,
Each to his Home, retire; save Those that love
To take their Pastime in the troubled Air,
Or skimming flutter round the dimply Pool.
The Cattle from th' untasted Fields return,
45   And ask, with meaning Lowe, their wonted Stalls,
Or ruminate in the contiguous Shade.
Thither the houshold feathery People croud,
The crested Cock, with all his female Train,
Pensive, and dripping; while the Cottage-Hind
50   Hangs o'er th' enlivening Blaze, and taleful there
Recounts his simple Frolick: much he talks,
And much he laughs, nor recks the Storm that blows
Without, and rattles on his humble Roof.

Wide o'er the Brim, with many a Torrent swell'd,
55   And the mix'd Ruin of its Banks o'erspread,
At last the rous'd-up River pours along:
Resistless, roaring, dreadful, down it comes,
From the rude Mountain, and the mossy Wild,

27 *Genius:* Spirit   **29** *brawling:* flowing noisily.
32 *the Father of the Tempest:* Winter.
43 *dimply:* dimpled (by rain-drops).
45 *meaning:* meaningful.   **46** *contiguous:* adjoining the cattle-shed.

Tumbling thro Rocks abrupt, and sounding far;
60 Then o'er the sanded Valley floating spreads,
Calm, sluggish, silent; till again constrain'd,
Between two meeting Hills it bursts a Way,
Where Rocks and Woods o'erhang the turbid Stream;
There gathering triple Force, rapid, and deep,
65 It boils, and wheels, and foams, and thunders thro.

Nature! great Parent! whose unceasing Hand
Rolls round the Seasons of the changeful Year,
How mighty, how majestic, are thy Works!
With what a pleasing Dread they swell the Soul!
70 That sees astonish'd! and astonish'd sings!
Ye too, ye Winds! that now begin to blow,
With boisterous Sweep, I raise my Voice to you.
Where are your Stores, ye powerful Beings! say,
Where your aërial Magazines reserv'd,
75 To swell the brooding Terrors of the Storm?
In what far-distant Region of the Sky,
Hush'd in deep Silence, sleep you when 'tis calm?

When from the palid Sky the Sun descends,
With many a Spot, that o'er his glaring Orb
80 Uncertain wanders, stain'd; red fiery Streaks
Begin to flush around. The reeling Clouds
Stagger with dizzy Poise, as doubting yet
Which Master to obey: while rising slow,
Blank, in the leaden-colour'd East, the Moon
85 Wears a wan Circle round her blunted Horns.
Seen thro the turbid fluctuating Air,
The Stars obtuse emit a shivering Ray;
Or frequent seem to shoot athwart the Gloom,

74 *Magazines:* supplies.
79 *Spot:* sunspot. Sunspots produce electrical storms.
82 *Poise:* uncertainty, state of indecision.
87 *obtuse:* dull, indistinct.
88-9 In December and January two of the principal meteor showers are to be seen—the Geminids and the Boötids.

And long behind them trail the whitening Blaze.
90   Snatch'd in short Eddies, plays the wither'd Leaf;
And on the Flood the dancing Feather floats.
With broaden'd Nostrils to the Sky upturn'd,
The conscious Heifer snuffs the stormy Gale.
Even as the Matron, at her nightly Task,
95   With pensive Labour draws the flaxen Thread,
The wasted Taper and the crackling Flame
Foretel the Blast. But chief the plumy Race,
The Tenants of the Sky, its Changes speak.
Retiring from the Downs, where all Day long
100   They pick'd their scanty Fare, a blackening Train
Of clamorous Rooks thick-urge their weary Flight,
And seek the closing Shelter of the Grove.
Assiduous, in his Bower, the wailing Owl
Plies his sad Song. The Cormorant on high
105   Wheels from the Deep, and screams along the Land.
Loud shrieks the soaring Hern; and with wild Wing
The circling Sea-Fowl cleave the flaky Clouds.
Ocean, unequal press'd, with broken Tide
And blind Commotion heaves; while from the Shore,
110   Eat into Caverns by the restless Wave,
And Forest-rustling Mountain, comes a Voice,
That solemn-sounding bids the World prepare.
Then issues forth the Storm with sudden Burst,
And hurls the whole precipitated Air,
115   Down, in a Torrent. On the passive Main
Descends th' etherial Force, and with strong Gust
Turns from its Bottom the discolour'd Deep.
Thro' the black Night that sits immense around,
Lash'd into Foam, the fierce conflicting Brine
120   Seems o'er a thousand raging Waves to burn;

101 *thick-urge:* An early and hurried return of crows to the rookery was supposed to be a sign of an approaching storm.
103 *Assiduous:* unremitting in his call.
106 *Hern:* heron.
110 *Eat:* eaten.
117 *discolour'd:* i.e. with disturbed sand and seaweed.

Meantime the Mountain-Billows, to the Clouds
In dreadful Tumult swell'd, Surge above Surge,
Burst into Chaos with tremendous Roar,
And anchor'd Navies from their Stations drive,
125   Wild as the Winds, across the howling Waste
Of mighty Waters: now th' inflated Wave
Straining they scale, and now impetuous shoot
Into the secret Chambers of the Deep,
The wintry Baltick thundering o'er their Head.
130   Emerging thence again, before the Breath
Of full-exerted Heaven they wing their Course,
And dart on distant Coasts; if some sharp Rock,
Or Shoal insidious break not their Career,
And in loose Fragments fling them floating round.

135   Nor less at Land the loosen'd Tempest reigns.
The Mountain thunders; and its sturdy Sons
Stoop to the Bottom of the Rocks they shade.
Lone on the midnight Steep, and all aghast,
The dark way-faring Stranger breathless toils,
140   And, often falling, climbs against the Blast.
Low waves the rooted Forest, vex'd, and sheds
What of its tarnish'd Honours yet remain;
Dash'd down, and scatter'd, by the tearing Wind's
Assiduous Fury, its gigantic Limbs.
145   Thus struggling thro' the dissipated Grove,
The whirling Tempest raves along the Plain;
And on the Cottage thatch'd, or lordly Roof,
Keen-fastening, shakes them to the solid Base.
Sleep frighted flies; and round the rocking Dome,
150   For Entrance eager, howls the savage Blast.
Then too, they say, thro all the burthen'd Air,
Long Groans are heard, shrill Sounds, and distant Sighs,

126 *inflated:* blown up by the wind.
136 *its sturdy Sons:* trees.
142 *Honours:* Cf. *Windsor-Forest* p. 52, l. 219.
145 *dissipated:* scattered.
149 *Dome:* house.

    That, utter'd by the Demon of the Night,
    Warn the devoted Wretch of Woe and Death.

155   Huge Uproar lords it wide. The Clouds commix'd
    With Stars swift-gliding sweep along the Sky.
    All Nature reels. Till Nature's KING, who oft
    Amid tempestuous Darkness dwells alone,
    And on the Wings of the careering Wind
160   Walks dreadfully serene, commands a Calm;
    Then straight Air Sea and Earth are hush'd at once.

    As yet 'tis Midnight deep. The weary Clouds,
    Slow-meeting, mingle into solid Gloom.
    Now, while the drowsy World lies lost in Sleep,
165   Let me associate with the serious *Night*,
    And *Contemplation*, her sedate Compeer;
    Let me shake off th' intrusive Cares of Day,
    And lay the meddling Senses all aside.

    Where now, ye lying Vanities of Life!
170   Ye ever-tempting ever-cheating Train!
    Where are you now? and what is your Amount?
    Vexation, Disappointment, and Remorse.
    Sad, sickening Thought! and yet deluded Man,
    A Scene of crude disjointed Visions past,
175   And broken Slumbers, rises still resolv'd,
    With new-flush'd Hopes, to run the giddy Round.

    FATHER of Light and Life! thou GOOD SUPREME!
    O teach me what is good! teach me THYSELF!
    Save me from Folly, Vanity, and Vice,
180   From every low Pursuit! and feed my Soul
    With Knowledge, conscious Peace, and Virtue pure,
    Sacred, substantial, never-fading Bliss!

154 *devoted:* doomed.
166 *Compeer:* companion.
176 *new-flush'd:* freshly animated. ("Flushed" can mean "set flying out of cover" as a dog flushes birds, but this does not fit well with what follows.)

    The keener Tempests come: and fuming dun
From all the livid East, or piercing North,
185 Thick Clouds ascend; in whose capacious Womb
A vapoury Deluge lies, to Snow congeal'd.
Heavy they roll their fleecy World along;
And the Sky saddens with the gather'd Storm.
Thro the hush'd Air the whitening Shower descends,
190 At first thin-wavering; till at last the Flakes
Fall broad, and wide, and fast, dimming the Day,
With a continual Flow. The cherish'd Fields
Put on their Winter-Robe, of purest White.
'Tis Brightness all; save where the new Snow melts,
195 Along the mazy Current. Low, the Woods
Bow their hoar Head; and, ere the languid Sun
Faint from the West emits his Evening-Ray,
Earth's universal Face, deep-hid, and chill,
Is one wild dazzling Waste, that buries wide
200 The Works of Man. Drooping, the Labourer-Ox
Stands cover'd o'er with Snow, and then demands
The Fruit of all his Toil. The Fowls of Heaven,
Tam'd by the cruel Season, croud around
The winnowing Store, and claim the little Boon
205 Which PROVIDENCE assigns them. One alone,
The Red-Breast, sacred to the houshold Gods,
Wisely regardful of th' embroiling Sky,
In joyless Fields, and Thorny Thickets, leaves
His shivering Mates, and pays to trusted Man
210 His annual Visit. Half-afraid, he first
Against the Window beats; then, brisk, alights
On the warm Hearth; then, hopping o'er the Floor,
Eyes all the smiling Family askance,
And pecks, and starts, and wonders where he is:
215 Till more familiar grown, the Table-Crumbs
Attract his slender Feet. The foodless Wilds
Pour forth their brown Inhabitants. The Hare,
Tho timorous of Heart, and hard beset

183 *dun:* brown, or gloomy.   184 *livid:* leaden-coloured.
204 *The winnowing Store:* the barn where chaff is separated from grain.

By Death in various Forms, dark Snares, and Dogs,
220   And more unpitying Men, the Garden seeks,
Urg'd on by fearless Want. The bleating Kind
Eye the bleak Heaven, and next the glistening Earth,
With Looks of dumb Despair; then, sad-dispersed,
Dig for the wither'd Herb thro Heaps of Snow.

225   Now, Shepherds, to your helpless Charge be kind,
Baffle the raging Year, and fill their Pens
With Food at Will; lodge them below the Storm,
And watch them strict: for from the bellowing East,
In this dire Season, oft the Whirlwind's Wing
230   Sweeps up the Burthen of whole wintry Plains
In one wide Waft, and o'er the hapless Flocks,
Hid in the Hollow of two neighbouring Hills,
The billowy Tempest whelms; till, upward urg'd,
The Valley to a shining Mountain swells,
235   Tipt with a Wreath, high-curling in the Sky.

As thus the Snows arise; and foul, and fierce,
All Winter drives along the darken'd Air;
In his own loose-revolving Fields, the Swain
Disaster'd stands; sees other Hills ascend,
240   Of unknown joyless Brow; and other Scenes,
Of horrid Prospect, shag the trackless Plain:
Nor finds the River, nor the Forest, hid
Beneath the formless Wild; but wanders on
From Hill to Dale, still more and more astray;
245   Impatient flouncing thro the drifted Heaps,
Stung with the Thoughts of Home; the Thoughts of Home
Rush on his Nerves, and call their Vigour forth
In many a vain Attempt. How sinks his Soul!
What black Despair, what Horror fills his Heart!
250   When for the dusky Spot, which Fancy feign'd

231 *Waft:* gust.
238 *loose-revolving:* seeming to whirl about him in the wind.
239 *Disaster'd:* stricken with calamity.
241 *shag:* cover with a rough, shaggy surface.   247 *Nerves:* sinews.

His tufted Cottage rising thro the Snow,
He meets the Roughness of the middle Waste,
Far from the Track, and blest Abode of Man;
While round him Night resistless closes fast,
255   And every Tempest, howling o'er his Head,
Renders the savage Wilderness more wild.
Then throng the busy Shapes into his Mind,
Of cover'd Pits, unfathomably deep,
A dire Descent! beyond the Power of Frost,
260   Of faithless Bogs; of Precipices huge,
Smooth'd up with Snow; and, what is Land unknown,
What Water, of the still unfrozen Spring,
In the loose Marsh or solitary Lake,
Where the fresh Fountain from the Bottom boils.
265   These check his fearful Steps; and down he sinks
Beneath the Shelter of the shapeless Drift,
Thinking o'er all the Bitterness of Death,
Mix'd with the tender Anguish Nature shoots
Thro the wrung Bosom of the dying Man,
270   His Wife, his Children, and his Friends unseen.
In vain for him th' officious Wife prepares
The Fire fair-blazing, and the Vestment warm;
In vain his little Children, peeping out
Into the mingling Storm, demand their Sire,
275   With Tears of artless Innocence. Alas!
Nor Wife, nor Children, more shall he behold,
Nor Friends, nor sacred Home. On every Nerve
The deadly Winter seizes; shuts up Sense;
And, o'er his inmost Vitals creeping cold,
280   Lays him along the Snows, a stiffen'd Corse,
Stretch'd out, and bleaching in the northern Blast.

251 *tufted:* often means "with trees grouped over it", but here "tufted"
may mean "thatched", or even "shaggy with snow".
259 *beyond the Power of Frost:* i.e. bogs which would not freeze over.
271 *officious:* dutiful.
280 *Corse:* corpse.

Edward Young

from NIGHT-THOUGHTS

IN 1740 it must have seemed that the great days of Edward Young (1683–1765), when he had been numbered with his friends, Pope and Addison, among the major poets of his time, were past. Yet his earlier reputation was quite overshadowed by the fame of *The Complaint: or, Night-Thoughts on Life, Death & Immortality*, published serially from 1742 to 1745. The poem's sombre moods, moral truths and Christian faith, suggestions of personal tragedy, and rhetorical energy caught the imagination of a public which liked its piety spiced with declamatory reproaches and visions. For a man who had written accomplished heroic couplets, Young's conversion to blank verse was whole-hearted:

> Blank is a term of diminution; what we mean by blank verse, is, verse unfallen, uncurst; verse reclaimed, reinthroned in the true language of the gods; who never thundered, nor suffered their Homer to thunder, in rhyme.

Night-Thoughts certainly has passages of thunderous eloquence; but whether the climate of Young's verse is too continuously stormy, or whether it too frequently sounds like the rumble of a thunder-sheet in the wings instead of the voice of the gods, this poem, once ranked among the masterpieces of our literature, is now read less often than the lively critical work, *Conjectures on Original Composition*, 1759 (from which the above sentence is taken).

The text is that of the first edition of 1742. I have not interfered with Young's idiosyncratic use of italics since it seems to be part of his emphatic stressing and frequent personification. Similarly I have not replaced his question-marks with exclamation-marks in lines 21, 61, 67–89, 115 and 121, because Young seems to be distinguishing between speculations and guesses ending with a question-mark and assertions ending with an exclamation-mark.

from THE COMPLAINT. NIGHT THE FIRST
(lines 1–133)

Tir'd nature's sweet Restorer, balmy *Sleep!*
He, like the World, his ready visit pays,
Where Fortune smiles; the wretched he forsakes:
Swift on his downy pinion flies from Woe,
5　And lights on Lids unsully'd with a Tear.
　　From short, (as usual) and disturb'd Repose,
I wake: How happy they who wake no more!
Yet that were vain, if Dreams infest the Grave.
I wake, emerging from a sea of Dreams
10　Tumultuous; where my wreck'd, desponding Thought
From wave to wave of *fancy'd* Misery,
At random drove, her helm of Reason lost;
Tho' now restor'd, 'tis only Change of pain,
A bitter change; severer for severe:
15　The *Day* too short for my Distress! and *Night*
Ev'n in the *Zenith* of her dark Domain,
Is Sun-shine, to the colour of my Fate.
　　Night, sable Goddess! from her *Ebon* throne,
In rayless Majesty, now stretches forth
20　Her leaden Scepter o'er a slumbering world:
Silence, how dead? and Darkness, how profound?
Nor Eye, nor list'ning Ear an object finds;
Creation sleeps. 'Tis, as the general Pulse
Of life stood still, and Nature made a Pause;
25　An aweful pause! prophetic of her End.
And let her prophecy be soon fulfil'd;
Fate! drop the Curtain; I can lose no more.
　　Silence, and *Darkness!* solemn Sisters! Twins
From antient *Night*, who nurse the tender Thought
30　To *Reason*; and on reason build *Resolve*,
(That column of true Majesty in man!)
Assist me: I will thank you in the Grave;

The grave, your Kingdom: *There* this Frame shall fall
A victim sacred to your dreary shrine:
35   But what are Ye? *Thou*, who didst put to flight
Primaeval *Silence*, when the Morning Stars
Exulting, shouted o'er the rising Ball;
O thou! whose Word from solid *Darkness* struck
That spark, the Sun; strike Wisdom from my soul;
40   My soul which flies to thee, her Trust, her Treasure;
As misers to their Gold, while others rest.
    Thro' this Opaque of Nature, and of Woe,
This double Night, transmit one pitying ray,
To lighten, and to chear: O lead my Mind,
45   (A Mind that fain would wander from its Woe,)
Lead it thro' various scenes of *Life* and *Death*,
And from each scene, the noblest Truths inspire:
Nor less inspire my *Conduct*, than my *Song*;
Teach my best Reason, Reason; my best Will
50   Teach Rectitude; and fix my firm Resolve
Wisdom to wed, and pay her long Arrear.
Nor let the vial of thy Vengeance pour'd
On this devoted head, be pour'd in vain.
    The Bell strikes *One*: We take no note of Time,
55   But from its Loss. To give it then a Tongue,
Is wise in man. As if an Angel spoke,
I feel the solemn Sound. If heard aright,
It is the *Knell* of my departed Hours;
Where are they? With the years beyond the Flood:
60   It is the *Signal* that demands Dispatch;
How Much is to be done? My Hopes and Fears
Start up alarm'd, and o'er life's narrow Verge
Look down—on what? a fathomless Abyss;
A dread Eternity! how surely *mine!*
65   And can Eternity belong to me,

34 *sacred:* consecrated.
36–7 God speaks (in *Job*, xxviii, 7) of the Creation as the time "when the morning stars sang together, and all the sons of God shouted for joy".
42 *Opaque:* utter darkness (here both of night and grief).
53 *devoted:* doomed, accurst.   **60** *Dispatch:* speed.

Poor Pensioner on the mercies of an Hour?
  How poor? how rich? how abject? how august?
How complicat? how wonderful is Man?
How passing wonder He, who made him such?
70 Who center'd in our make such strange Extremes?
From different Natures, marvelously mixt,
Connection exquisite of distant Worlds!
Distinguisht *Link* in Being's endless Chain!
Midway from *Nothing* to the *Deity!*
75 A Beam etherial sully'd, and absorpt!
Tho' sully'd, and dishonour'd, still Divine!
Dim Miniature of Greatness absolute!
An Heir of Glory! a frail Child of Dust!
Helpless Immortal! Insect *infinite!*
80 A Worm! a God! I tremble at myself,
And in myself am lost! at home a Stranger,
Thought wanders up and down, surpriz'd, amaz'd,
And wond'ring at her *own:* How Reason reels?
O what a Miracle to man is man,
85 Triumphantly distrest? what Joy, what Dread?
Alternately transported, and alarm'd!
What can preserve my Life? or what destroy?
An Angel's arm can't snatch me from the Grave;
Legions of Angels can't confine me There.
90 'Tis past Conjecture; all things rise in Proof:
While o'er my limbs *Sleep*'s soft dominion spread,

67 This is only one of many places in *Night-Thoughts* where Shakespeare's plays, especially *Hamlet*, seem to be at the back of Young's mind. But the subsequent antitheses seem to be more indebted to Pope's *Essay on Man*, II. 1–18.

68 *Complicat:* complex.

73 *Being's endless Chain:* The dominant concept of the universal order during the eighteenth century (and for many centuries before) was of a "Great Chain of Being". Every kind of existence that could exist did exist, forming an unbroken chain from the merest sub-microscopic specks of life to the highest orders of angels or God himself. Man was the creature who formed the middle-link of this chain—part spiritual and part animal.

75 The spiritual ray in man is stained by its incorporation in flesh.

What, tho' my soul phantastic Measures trod,
O'er Fairy Fields; or mourn'd along the gloom
Of pathless Woods; or down the craggy Steep
95 Hurl'd headlong, swam with pain the mantled Pool;
Or scal'd the Cliff; or danc'd on hollow Winds,
With antic Shapes, wild Natives of the Brain?
Her ceaseless Flight, tho' devious, speaks her Nature,
Of subtler Essence than the trodden Clod;
100 Active, aerial, tow'ring, unconfin'd,
Unfetter'd with her gross Companion's fall:
Ev'n silent Night proclaims my soul immortal:
Ev'n silent Night proclaims eternal Day:
For human weal, Heaven husbands all events,
105 Dull Sleep instructs, nor sport vain Dreams in vain.
    Why then *their* Loss deplore, that are not lost?
Why wanders wretched Thought their tombs around,
In infidel distress? Are *Angels* there?
Slumbers, rak'd up in dust, Etherial fire?
110 They live! they greatly live a life on earth
Unkindled, unconceiv'd; and from an eye
Of Tenderness, let heav'nly pity fall,
On me, more justly number'd with the Dead:
This is the Desert, *this* the Solitude;
115 How populous? how vital, is the Grave?
This is Creation's melancholy Vault,
The Vale funereal, the sad *Cypress* gloom;
The land of Apparitions, empty Shades:
All, all on earth is *Shadow*, all beyond
120 Is *Substance*; the reverse is Folly's *creed*;
How solid all, where Change shall be no more?

95 *pain:* distress, difficulty.   *mantled:* covered with scum.
96 *hollow Winds:* Cf. *Windsor-Forest*, p. 46, l. 68.
97 *antic:* grotesque.
100 *tow'ring:* Cf. "A Night-Piece on Death", p. 85, l. 89.
101 *her gross Companion's fall:* the death of the body.
104 *husbands:* makes good use of.
    117 *Cypress:* Branches of the cypress tree were used at funerals as symbols
of mourning. Cf. "A Night-Piece on Death", p. 84, l. 72.

This is the bud of Being, the dim Dawn,
The twilight of our Day; the Vestibule,
Life's Theater as yet is shut, and Death,
125 Strong Death alone can heave the massy Bar,
This gross impediment of Clay remove,
And make us Embryos of Existence free.
From *real* life, but little more remote
Is *He*, not yet a candidate for Light,
130 The *future* Embryo, slumbering in his Sire.
Embryos we must be, till we burst the Shell,
Yon ambient, azure shell, and spring to Life,
The life of Gods: O Transport! and of Man.

125 *massy Bar:* Young probably has in mind the heavy barrier which was raised when a theatre was opened.

128-130 The child not yet conceived is not much farther from real life (i.e. the life after death) than we are.

132 *Yon ambient, azure shell:* that encompassing blue sky, like a shell round the human embryonic spirit.

Robert Blair

from THE GRAVE

ROBERT BLAIR (1699-1746) was a Scottish clergyman of cheerful disposition who wrote little besides *The Grave*, in which, after some introductory freezing of the blood, he showed the corruption in death of all that men value, opened into a more general view of death's terrors, denounced sin, and concluded by warning death of the coming resurrection. His vivid insistence on physical and spiritual horrors, his declamatory energy, and a certain imaginative liveliness, joined to his pious intent, won him a very considerable reputation, little of which remains. Yet his blank verse moves dramatically, if sometimes melodramatically, and there are a number of appropriately forceful and evocative passages—for instance, the lines on a state funeral:

Great Gluts of People
Retard the unwieldy Show; whilst from the Casements
And Houses' Tops, ranks behind ranks close wedg'd
Hang bellying over.

The passage below consists of the first 71 lines of *The Grave* (1743): few readers now share the opinion of some of Blair's contemporaries that the poem of 767 lines was too short for its subject.

(lines 1–71)

Whilst some affect the Sun, and some the Shade,
Some flee the City, some the Hermitage;
Their Aims as various, as the Roads they take
In Journeying thro' Life; the Task be mine
5   To paint the gloomy Horrors of the *Tomb*;
Th' appointed Place of Rendezvous, where all
These Travellers meet. Thy Succours I implore,
Eternal King! whose potent Arm sustains
The Keys of Hell and Death. THE GRAVE, dread Thing!
10   Men shiver, when thou'rt nam'd: Nature appall'd
Shakes off her wonted Firmness. Ah! how dark
Thy long-extended Realms, and rueful Wastes!
Where nought but Silence reigns, and Night, dark Night,
Dark as was *Chaos*, 'ere the Infant Sun
15   Was roll'd together, or had try'd his Beams
Athwart the Gloom profound! The sickly Taper
By glimmering thro' thy low-brow'd misty Vaults,
(Furr'd round with mouldy Damps, and ropy Slime,)
Lets fall a supernumerary Horror,
20   And only serves to make thy Night more irksome.
Well do I know thee by thy trusty *Yew*,
Chearless, unsocial Plant! that loves to dwell
'Midst Sculls and Coffins, Epitaphs and Worms:
Where light-heel'd Ghosts, and visionary Shades,
25   Beneath the wan cold Moon (as Fame reports)
Embody'd, thick, perform their mystick Rounds.
No other Merriment, Dull Tree! is thine.

See yonder Hallow'd Fane! the pious Work
Of Names once fam'd, now dubious or forgot,

1 *affect:* seek after, prefer.   12 *rueful:* dismal.
18 *ropy:* composed of sticky or slimy threads.
24 *visionary:* Cf. "A Night-Piece on Death", p. 84, l. 50.
28 *Fane:* church.   29 *dubious:* known uncertainly.

30   And buried 'midst the Wreck of Things which were:
      There lie interr'd the more illustrious Dead.
      The Wind is up: Hark! how it howls! Methinks
      Till now, I never heard a Sound so dreary:
      Doors creak, and Windows clap, and Night's foul Bird
35   Rook'd in the Spire screams loud: the gloomy Isles
      Black-plaster'd, and hung round with Shreds of 'Scutcheons
      And tatter'd Coats of Arms, send back the Sound
      Laden with heavier Airs, from the low Vaults
      The Mansions of the Dead. Rous'd from their Slumbers
40   In grim Array the grizly Spectres rise,
      Grin horrible, and obstinately sullen
      Pass and repass, hush'd as the Foot of Night.
      Again! the Screech-Owl shrieks: Ungracious Sound!
      I'll hear no more, it makes one's Blood run chill.

45   Quite round the Pile, a Row of Reverend Elms,
      Coæval near with that, all ragged shew,
      Long lash'd by the rude Winds: Some rift half down
      Their branchless Trunks: Others so thin a Top,
      That scarce Two Crows could lodge in the same Tree.
50   Strange Things, the Neighbours say, have happen'd here:
      Wild Shrieks have issu'd from the hollow Tombs,
      Dead men have come again, and walk'd about,
      And the Great Bell has toll'd, unrung, untouch'd.
      (Such Tales their Chear, at Wake or Gossiping,
55   When it draws near to Witching Time of Night.)

34 *Night's foul Bird:* the screech-owl.

35 *Rook'd:* a Scotticism: *rouked*—"crouched, lying close".   *Isles:* aisles.

36 *'Scutcheons:* Cf. *Trivia,* p. 73, l. 231.   **48** *a Top:* at the top.

54 *Gossiping:* This noun is not in the O.E.D., but the pairing with "Wake" (a funeral feast) suggests that it may mean "a baptismal feast", a gossip being a sponsor in baptism. But a "gossip" could also be a drinking companion. Perhaps any occasion when cronies sit up late drinking and talking may be meant.

55 *Witching Time of Night:* the time for supernatural phenomena. Cf. "Tis now the verie witching time of night" (*Hamlet,* iii, 2). A naïve but enthusiastic critic once wrote of Blair that "many of his expressions might pass and have passed for bits of Hamlet".

Oft, in the lone Church-yard at Night I've seen,
By Glimpse of Moon-shine chequering thro' the Trees,
The School-boy with his Satchel in his Hand,
Whistling aloud to bear his Courage up,
60   And lightly tripping o'er the long flat Stones
(With Nettles skirted, and with Moss o'ergrown,)
That tell in homely Phrase who lie below;
Sudden! he starts, and hears, or thinks he hears
The Sound of something purring at his Heels:
65   Full fast he flies, and dares not look behind him,
Till out of Breath he overtakes his Fellows;
Who gather round, and wonder at the Tale
Of horrid *Apparition*, tall and ghastly,
That walks at Dead of Night, or takes his Stand
70   O'er some new-open'd *Grave*; and, strange to tell!
Evanishes at Crowing of the Cock.

71 Here, too, the indebtedness to the ghost of Hamlet's father, who
"faded on the crowing of the cock" (i, 2), is obvious.

Joseph Warton

TO EVENING

THE literary importance of the criticism and poetry of Joseph Warton
(1722–1800) and his brother Thomas was not that of revolutionaries, but
of men who exemplified and made explicit certain trends in taste and
opinion which had been developing for half a century. The experience of
the natural scene seems fresh and first-hand, yet the careful management of
soft assonance and alliteration belongs to long-established notions of the
poet's art, as do the classical names and personifications and other accoutre-
ments of the nocturnal. What can be sensed as new is the assumption that to
evoke the mood and atmosphere of evening is enough, without searching
for appropriate meditations. For Warton, in this poem and in others,
"pensive" is a word referring to feelings rather than thoughts.
    "To Evening" is from *Odes on Various Subjects* (1746).

Hail meek-ey'd maiden, clad in sober grey,
Whose soft approach the weary woodman loves,
As homeward bent to kiss his prattling babes,
He jocund whistles thro' the twilight groves.

5 When PHOEBUS sinks behind the gilded hills,
You lightly o'er the misty meadows walk,
The drooping daisies bathe in honey-dews,
And nurse the nodding violet's slender stalk:

The panting Dryads, that in day's fierce heat
10 To inmost bowers and cooling caverns ran,
Return to trip in wanton evening-dances,
Old SYLVAN too returns, and laughing PAN.

To the deep wood the clamorous rooks repair,
Light skims the swallow o'er the wat'ry scene,
15 And from the sheep-cotes, and fresh-furrow'd field,
Stout plowmen meet to wrestle on the green.

The swain that artless sings on yonder rock,
His supping sheep and lengthening shadow spies,
Pleas'd with the cool, the calm, refreshful hour,
20 And with hoarse hummings of unnumber'd flies.

Now every passion sleeps; desponding Love,
And pining Envy, ever-restless Pride,
And holy calm creeps o'er my peaceful soul,
Anger and mad Ambition's storms subside.

25 O modest EVENING, oft' let me appear
A wandering votary in thy pensive train,
List'ning to every wildly-warbling throat
That fills with farewell notes the dark'ning plain.

---

5 PHOEBUS: Cf. "Grongar Hill", p. 88, l. 11.

7 *honey-dews:* a sweet sticky substance on plants, either exuded or deposited by aphides. As the word suggests, it was once thought that it was deposited from the air like dew.

9 *Dryads:* wood-nymphs.

11 *wanton:* probably "sportive, frolicsome", rather than "lascivious".

12 SYLVAN . . . PAN: Cf. *Cooper's Hill*, p. 33, l. 235, and *Windsor-Forest*, p. 51, l. 181.   26 *votary:* worshipper.

William Collins

ODE TO EVENING

THE "Ode to Evening" is demonstrably derivative in verse-form (borrowed from Milton's version of Horace's ode "To Pyrrha"), diction, imagery, mood and theme, and yet original in the only sense that really matters—nothing else quite like it is to be found in our literature. As Coleridge's imagination digested books, so that when he was writing "The Rime of the Ancient Mariner" images and phrases from his reading came unsought and transmuted to his mind, so for Collins the direct experience and the literary experience of nature seem to have been almost inseparable. Literature shaped his imagination without destroying its uniqueness. What he read and what he experienced were absorbed, united, and given a character peculiar to the poet. Yet though much of this process must have been unconscious, the "Ode to Evening" is far from being a piece of "unpremeditated art". The "soften'd Strain" which Collins required was partly achieved by consummate art: the long-drawn-out sentences interrupted by parentheses (despite some rhetorical full-stops, the poem consists essentially of only three complete sense units of 20, 20 and 12 lines respectively), the repeated "dying falls" at the ends of lines and quatrains, the subtle and complex alliteration and assonance, the echoes, inverted echoes, repetitions and hesitations, all contribute to the slow, vaguely melancholy, hushed music, in which evening is not so much described or presented, as somehow present.

The text is that of the first edition of *Odes on Several Descriptive and Allegoric Subjects* (1747).

If ought of Oaten Stop, or Pastoral Song,
  May hope, O pensive *Eve*, to sooth thine Ear,
    Like thy own brawling Springs,
    Thy Springs, and dying Gales,
5 O *Nymph* reserv'd, while now the bright-hair'd Sun

1 *Oaten Stop:* a musical pipe made out of an oat-straw. Cf. "Or sound of pastoral reed with oaten stops" (Milton: *Comus*, l. 345).

3 *brawling:* making a noisy passage across pebbles.

4 *Gales:* breezes.

Sits in yon western Tent, whose cloudy Skirts,
   With Brede ethereal wove,
   O'erhang his wavy Bed:
Now Air is hush'd, save where the weak-ey'd Bat,
10 With short shrill Shriek flits by on leathern Wing,
   Or where the Beetle winds
   His small but sullen Horn,
As oft he rises 'midst the twilight Path,
Against the Pilgrim born in heedless Hum:
15   Now teach me, *Maid* compos'd,
   To breathe some soften'd Strain,
Whose Numbers stealing thro' thy darkning Vale,
May not unseemly with its Stillness suit,
   As musing slow, I hail
20   Thy genial lov'd Return!
For when thy folding Star arising shews
His paly Circlet, at his warning Lamp
   The fragrant *Hours*, and *Elves*
   Who slept in Buds the Day,
25 And many a *Nymph* who wreaths her Brows with Sedge,
And sheds the fresh'ning dew, and lovelier still,
   The *Pensive Pleasures* sweet
   Prepare thy shadowy Car.
Then let me rove some wild and heathy Scene,
30 Or find some Ruin 'midst its dreary Dells,
   Whose Walls more awful nod
   By thy religious Gleams.

7 *Brede:* braid, ornately-woven band of material.

11–12 Cf. "What time the Gray-fly winds her sultry horn" (Milton: "Lycidas", 28). The echo of "sultry" in "sullen" suggests how Milton's poetry was sounding at the back of Collins's mind. But the succession of "bat-beetle-hum" is reminiscent also of *Macbeth* III, ii, 40–3. In *Poor Collins* (1937), E. G. Ainsworth Jr. has tried to list all Collins's echoes of Milton, Spenser, Shakespeare, Pope, Joseph Warton, and other poets.

17 *Numbers:* here, poetic sounds.   20 *genial:* pleasantly warm and mild.

21 *thy folding Star:* the evening star, which tells the shepherd it is time to return his sheep to their fold. Cf. "The Star that bids the Shepherd fold" (Milton: *Comus*, l. 93).

Or if chill blustring Winds, or driving Rain,
Prevent my willing Feet, be mine the Hut,

35   That from the Mountain's Side,
        Views Wilds, and swelling Floods,
And Hamlets brown, and dim-discover'd Spires,
And hears their simple Bell, and marks o'er all
        Thy Dewy Fingers draw

40   The gradual dusky Veil.
While *Spring* shall pour his Show'rs, as oft he wont,
And bathe thy breathing tresses, meekest *Eve*!
        While *Summer* loves to sport,
        Beneath thy ling'ring Light:

45 While sallow *Autumn* fills thy Lap with Leaves,
Or *Winter* yelling thro' the troublous Air,
        Affrights thy shrinking Train,
        And rudely rends thy Robes.
So long regardful of thy quiet Rule,

50   Shall *Fancy*, *Friendship*, *Science*, smiling *Peace*,
        Thy gentlest Influence own,
        And love thy fav'rite Name!

41 *as oft he wont:* as he is often wont to do.
42 *breathing:* fragrant.   **50** *Science:* knowledge, all learning.
52 *fav'rite:* i.e. Evening is the time of day especially beloved by and appropriate to the imagination, etc.

Thomas Gray

AN ODE ON A
DISTANT PROSPECT OF ETON COLLEGE

MANY reasons have been offered for the smallness of Gray's poetic output, but the obvious one is that he was a perfectionist, never satisfied until he had traced the roots of his personal experiences in universal experience, and had found for his thoughts and images, not only the right words, but their proper places in a process of thought, feeling and poetry.

Nothing in the opening of the Eton College ode (1747) warns us of the black view of human fate to which the train of thought and association will lead. The formal, stately language, the dignified apostrophes, the patterned syntax conceal the faint hints of pain and weariness in the second stanza, and, even when the carefree activities of the boys in the playing-fields are particularised, the language remains abstract and, as it were, detached. The shock of finding these gay creatures described as "little Victims" comes consequently with doubled force, and, at once, the whole current of the poem is deflected to the simple but terrible line, "Ah, tell them they are Men". Now everything is transformed: space and time melt together; the Thames Valley becomes "the Vale of Years"; "Gay Hope" becomes "Grim-visag'd, comfortless Despair"; the tears, once easily forgotten, are mocked by unkindness; "Wild Wit" is transformed to "moody Madness laughing wild" and "buxom Health" to pain-racked sickness. And then, as though this shift in the course and temper of the poem were not enough, there is even greater terror in Gray's withdrawal of his plea that the boys should be warned of what awaits them: their paradise is brief but nothing can preserve it or avert the sufferings, and the recollection of the first Fall in the Garden of Eden seems to find in man's very origins and nature his terrible destiny.

The *Elegy* (1751) has a similar, though less shocking, coherence. The falling darkness in the opening stanzas leads naturally to the graves immediately around, thus to "the short and simple annals of the poor", and then (through the negatives of the stanza which begins "Let not Ambition mock their useful Toil") to the monumental tombs of the great. Gray was a master of the transition, and here we are taken from a small country churchyard to the interior of a great cathedral in a natural progression, which was perhaps the reason why Gray asked for his poem to be printed without breaks between the quatrains. This movement establishes the central contrast between the honoured and unhonoured dead, culminating in the passage where both are seen as motivated by the same natural yearning to be remembered—the passage of which Dr. Johnson wrote: "The four stanzas beginning 'Yet even these bones' are to me original: I have never seen the notions in any other place; yet he that reads them here persuades himself that he has always felt them." After this, Gray's vision of his own unfulfilled life (very much in the spirit of Milton's "Lycidas" or Keats's sonnet "When I have fears that I may cease to be") quietly returns to the solitary poet left in darkness at the beginning of the poem.

The texts of the first editions have been exactly followed, save in l. 27 of the *Elegy*, where the word *they* was duplicated.

Ye distant Spires, ye antique Towers;
That crown the watry Glade,

Where grateful Science still adores
Her Henry's holy Shade;
5   And ye that from the stately Brow
Of Windsor's Heights th' Expanse below
Of Grove, of Lawn, of Mead survey,
Whose Turf, whose Shade, whose Flowers among
Wanders the hoary Thames along
10   His Silver-winding Way.

Ah happy Hills, ah pleasing Shade,
Ah Fields belov'd in vain,
Where once my careless Childhood stray'd,
A Stranger yet to Pain!
15   I feel the Gales, that from ye blow,
A momentary Bliss bestow,
As waving fresh their gladsome Wing,
My weary Soul they seem to sooth,
And, redolent of Joy and Youth,
20   To breathe a second Spring.

Say, Father Thames, for thou hast seen
Full many a sprightly Race
Disporting on thy Margent green
The Paths of Pleasure trace,
25   Who foremost now delight to cleave
With pliant Arm thy glassy Wave?
The captive Linnet which enthrall?
What idle Progeny succeed
To chase the rolling Circle's Speed,
30   Or urge the flying Ball?

While some on earnest Business bent
Their murm'ring Labours ply,

3 *Science:* Cf. "Ode to Evening", p. 124, l. 50.
4 *Henry:* Henry VI, the founder of Eton College, whose statue stands in the school yard.
13 *careless:* carefree.   15 *Gales:* breezes.   23 *Margent:* bank.
28 *succeed:* come now in succession.   29 *the rolling Circle:* hoop.

'Gainst graver Hours, that bring Constraint
To sweeten Liberty:
35   Some bold Adventurers disdain
The Limits of their little Reign,
And unknown Regions dare descry:
Still as they run they look behind,
They hear a Voice in every Wind,
40   And snatch a fearful Joy.

Gay Hope is theirs by Fancy fed,
Less pleasing when possest;
The Tear forgot as soon as shed,
The Sunshine of the Breast,
45   Theirs buxom Health of rosy Hue,
Wild Wit, Invention ever-new,
And lively Chear of Vigour born;
The thoughtless Day, the easy Night,
The Spirits pure, the Slumbers light,
50   That fly th' Approach of Morn.

Alas, regardless of their Doom,
The little Victims play!
No Sense have they of Ills to come,
Nor Care beyond to-day:
55   Yet see how all around 'em wait
The Ministers of human Fate,
And black Misfortune's baleful Train!
Ah, shew them where in Ambush stand
To seize their Prey the murth'rous Band!
60   Ah, tell them they are Men!

These shall the Fury Passions tear,
The Vulturs of the Mind,
Disdainful Anger, pallid Fear,

35–6 *disdain The Limits:* break bounds.
   41–2 It is not the hope which is less pleasing when possessed but the thing hoped for.

And Shame that sculks behind;
65   Or pineing Love shall waste their Youth,
Or jealousy with rankling Tooth,
That inly gnaws the secret Heart,
And Envy wan, and faded Care,
Grim-visag'd comfortless Despair,
70   And Sorrow's piercing Dart.

Ambition This shall tempt to rise,
Then whirl the Wretch from high,
To bitter Scorn a Sacrifice,
And grinning Infamy.
75   The Stings of Falshood Those shall try,
And hard Unkindness' alter'd Eye,
That mocks the Tear it forc'd to flow;
And keen Remorse with Blood defil'd,
And moody Madness laughing wild
80   Amid severest Woe.

Lo, in the Vale of Years beneath
A griesly Troop are seen,
The painful Family of Death,
More hideous than their Queen:
85   This racks the Joints, this fires the Veins,
That every labouring Sinew strains,
Those in the deeper Vitals rage:
Lo, Poverty, to fill the Band,
That numbs the Soul with icy Hand,
90   And slow-consuming Age.

To each his Suff'rings: all are Men,
Condemn'd alike to groan,
The Tender for another's Pain;
Th' Unfeeling for his own.
95   Yet ah! Why should they know their Fate?
Since Sorrow never comes too late,
And Happiness too swiftly flies.

70 *Dart:* a spear.

Thought would destroy their Paradise.
No more; where Ignorance is Bliss,
100 'Tis Folly to be wise.

98–100 The allusion is to the loss of Paradise through Adam and Eve's having eaten the apple from the tree of knowledge of Good and Evil. The story was often used as a type of the loss of childhood innocence in every person's life, but Gray gets a bitterer flavour by suggesting that what is lost is ignorance (i.e. unawareness) which is all that makes man's lot bearable.

AN ELEGY WROTE IN A COUNTRY CHURCH YARD

The *Curfeu* tolls the Knell of parting Day,
The lowing Herd winds slowly o'er the Lea,
The Plow-man homeward plods his weary Way,
And leaves the World to Darkness, and to me.
5   Now fades the glimmering Landscape on the Sight,
And all the Air a solemn Stillness holds;
Save where the Beetle wheels his droning Flight,
And drowsy Tinklings lull the distant Folds.
Save that from yonder Ivy-mantled Tow'r
10 The mopeing Owl does to the Moon complain
Of such, as wand'ring near her sacred Bow'r,
Molest her ancient solitary Reign.
Beneath those rugged Elms, that Yew-Tree's Shade,
Where heaves the Turf in many a mould'ring Heap,
15 Each in his narrow Cell for ever laid,
The rude Forefathers of the Hamlet sleep.

1 *Curfeu:* Although the curfew (*couvre-feu*) bell had lost its original significance as the signal for the extinguishing of all lights and fires, the name was retained for the evening bell.

6 *Stillness:* the subject of the verb. **11** *sacred:* later corrected to "secret".

15 *narrow Cell:* specifically, "grave". But a "narrow cell" could be any small one-roomed dwelling. Gray is using words which could apply to both living and dead villagers, to prepare for the contrast between those who will wake from their sleep and those who will not. Cf. "lowly" (l. 20).

16 *rude:* uncultivated.

The breezy Call of Incense-breathing Morn,
The Swallow twitt'ring from the Straw-built Shed,
The Cock's shrill Clarion, or the ecchoing Horn,
20 No more shall wake them from their lowly Bed.

For them no more the blazing Hearth shall burn,
Or busy Houswife ply her Evening Care:
No Children run to lisp their Sire's Return,
Or climb his Knees the envied Kiss to share.

25 Oft did the Harvest to their Sickle yield,
Their Furrow oft the stubborn Glebe has broke;
How jocund did they drive their Team afield!
How bow'd the Woods beneath their sturdy Stroke!

Let not Ambition mock their useful Toil,
30 Their homely Joys and Destiny obscure;
Nor Grandeur hear with a disdainful Smile,
The short and simple Annals of the Poor.

The Boast of Heraldry, the Pomp of Pow'r,
And all that Beauty, all that Wealth e'er gave,
35 Awaits alike th' inevitable Hour.
The Paths of Glory lead but to the Grave.

Forgive, ye Proud, th' involuntary Fault,
If Memory to these no Trophies raise,
Where thro' the long-drawn Isle and fretted Vault
40 The pealing Anthem swells the Note of Praise.

Can storied Urn or animated Bust
Back to its Mansion call the fleeting Breath?
Can Honour's Voice provoke the silent Dust,
Or Flatt'ry sooth the dull cold Ear of Death!

17 *Incense-breathing:* fragrant. Cf. "Ode to Evening", p. 124, l. 42.
20 *lowly:* (i) low, i.e. beneath the ground, and (ii) humble.
22 *Care:* duties.   **26** *Glebe:* here, "soil".   **27** *afield:* to the field.
35 *Hour:* the subject of "awaits". Appropriately it waits at the end of the sentence.
39 *Isle:* aisle.   *fretted Vault:* high arched roof, ornamented with an interlacing pattern.
41 *storied:* Gray is thinking of an urn bearing an inscription telling of the "historical" achievement of the dead.
43 *provoke:* summon.

45   Perhaps in this neglected Spot is laid
      Some Heart once pregnant with celestial Fire,
      Hands that the Reins of Empire might have sway'd,
      Or wak'd to Extacy the living Lyre.
            But Knowledge to their Eyes her ample Page
50   Rich with the Spoils of Time did ne'er unroll;
      Chill Penury repress'd their noble Rage,
      And froze the genial Current of the Soul.
            Full many a Gem of purest Ray serene,
      The dark unfathom'd Caves of Ocean bear:
55   Full many a Flower is born to blush unseen,
      And waste its Sweetness on the desart Air.
            Some Village-Hampden that with dauntless Breast
      The little Tyrant of his Fields withstood;
      Some mute inglorious Milton here may rest,
60   Some Cromwell guiltless of his Country's Blood.
            Th' Applause of list'ning Senates to command,
      The Threats of Pain and Ruin to despise,
      To scatter Plenty o'er a smiling Land,
      And read their Hist'ry in a Nation's Eyes
65   Their Lot forbad: nor circumscrib'd alone
      Their growing Virtues, but their Crimes confin'd;
      Forbad to wade through Slaughter to a Throne,
      And shut the Gates of Mercy on Mankind,
            The struggling Pangs of conscious Truth to hide,
70   To quench the Blushes of ingenuous Shame,
      Or heap the Shrine of Luxury and Pride
      With Incense, kindled at the Muse's Flame.
            Far from the madding Crowd's ignoble Strife,
      Their sober Wishes never learn'd to stray;
75   Along the cool sequester'd Vale of Life
      They kept the noiseless Tenor of their Way.

    51 *Rage:* fervour, inspiration.   **52** *genial:* favourable to growth.
    57 *Hampden:* John Hampden, a Buckinghamshire squire, resisted what
he regarded as the tyrannous taxation of Charles I.
    65 *circumscrib'd:* This is a finite verb governed by the subject "Lot", as
are "confin'd" (l. 66) and "Forbad" (l. 67).
    71–2 i.e. to flatter with panegyrical poetry.
    73 *madding:* frenzied, confusedly hastening about. **76** *Tenor:* steady course.

      Yet ev'n these Bones from Insult to protect
Some frail Memorial still erected nigh,
With uncouth Rhimes and shapeless Sculpture deck'd,
80   Implores the passing Tribute of a Sigh.
      Their Name, their Years, spelt by th' unletter'd Muse,
The Place of Fame and Elegy supply:
And many a holy Text around she strews,
That teach the rustic Moralist to dye.
85   For who to dumb Forgetfulness a Prey,
This pleasing anxious Being e'er resign'd,
Left the warm Precincts of the chearful Day,
Nor cast one longing ling'ring Look behind!
      On some fond Breast the parting Soul relies,
90   Some pious Drops the closing Eye requires;
Ev'n from the Tomb the Voice of Nature cries
Awake, and faithful to her wonted Fires.
      For thee, who mindful of th' unhonour'd Dead
Dost in these Lines their artless Tale relate;
95   If chance, by lonely Contemplation led,
Some hidden Spirit shall inquire thy Fate,
      Haply some hoary-headed Swain may say,
'Oft have we seen him at the Peep of Dawn
'Brushing with hasty Steps the Dews away
100 'To meet the Sun upon the upland Lawn.
      'There at the Foot of yonder nodding Beech
'That wreathes its old fantastic Roots so high,
'His listless Length at Noontide wou'd he stretch,
'And pore upon the Brook that babbles by.

79 *uncouth:* clumsy.   **81** *unletter'd:* unlearned.

91 *Nature:* here, "human nature"—"What is true of all men, at all times, and in all places".

92 *Fires:* emotions, passions.

93-6 There has been much critical discussion of the interpretation of these lines, but, as it is the poet himself who has been "mindful of th' unhonoured Dead", it seems most probable that he is here addressing himself, considering what could be said of him if he were to die young, and returning the poem to the personal note with which it began.

100 *Lawn:* glade.

105   'Hard by yon Wood, now frowning as in Scorn,
       'Mutt'ring his wayward Fancies he wou'd rove,
       'Now drooping, woeful wan, like one forlorn,
       'Or craz'd with Care, or cross'd in hopeless Love.
           'One Morn I miss'd him on the custom'd Hill,
110   'Along the Heath, and near his fav'rite Tree;
       'Another came; nor yet beside the Rill,
       'Nor up the Lawn, nor at the Wood was he.
           'The next with Dirges due in sad Array
       'Slow thro' the Church-way Path we saw him born.
115   'Approach and read (for thou can'st read) the Lay,
       'Grav'd on the Stone beneath yon aged Thorn.'

The EPITAPH

HERE rests his Head upon the Lap of Earth
A Youth to Fortune and to Fame unknown:
Fair Science frown'd not on his humble Birth,
120   *And Melancholy mark'd him for her own.*
           Large was his Bounty, and his Soul sincere,
       Heav'n did a Recompence as largely send:
       He gave to Mis'ry all he had, a Tear:
       He gain'd from Heav'n ('twas all he wish'd) a Friend.
125   *No farther seek his Merits to disclose,*
       Or draw his Frailties from their dread Abode,
       (There they alike in trembling Hope repose)
       The Bosom of his Father and his God.

115 (*for thou can'st read*): The old peasant is, of course, illiterate.
119 *Science*: learning.
124 *a Friend*: Richard West, whose death in 1742, provided the impulse
for the Eton College ode, and perhaps for the first attempts at the *Elegy*.

Thomas Warton

THE FIRST OF APRIL

LIKE his brother Joseph, Thomas Warton (1728–90) was in the thick of most literary activities of the middle and late eighteenth century. He was poet, antiquarian, historian, editor, critic, biographer and literary historian; became, like his father before him, professor of poetry at Oxford; and in 1785 was made poet-laureate. But although his *History of English Poetry* was an important and influential work, he never fully achieved as a poet the promise he sometimes showed, as though his literary energies were dissipated in too many directions. Nevertheless, he is, at his best, a better poet than the current neglect of his work suggests: despite the relish of self-induced emotional states, *The Pleasures of Melancholy* (1747) was a remarkable achievement for a boy of nineteen, and has many fine and sounding passages, and the landscape of "The First of April" is charged with freshness and light.

The text is from *Poems. A New Edition, with Additions* (1777).

> With dalliance rude young Zephyr woos
> Coy May. Full oft with kind excuse
> The boisterous boy the Fair denies,
> Or, with a scornful smile, complies.
> 5   Mindful of disaster past,
> And shrinking at the northern blast,
> The sleety storm returning still,
> The morning hoar, and evening chill;
> Reluctant comes the timid Spring.
> 10 Scarce a bee, with airy ring,
> Murmurs the blossom'd boughs around,
> That cloath the garden's southern bound:
> Scarce a sickly straggling flower
> Decks the rough castle's rifted tower:

1 *Zephyr:* the god of the west wind.

2 *May:* a Roman spring goddess. Warton is thinking of the season, not the month. Zephyr's amorous attentions were usually paid to Flora (l. 23), the goddess of flowers and plants.

15 Scarce the hardy primrose peeps
From the dark dell's entangled steeps:
O'er the field of waving broom
Slowly shoots the golden bloom:
And, but by fits, the furze-clad dale
20 Tinctures the transitory gale.
While from the shrubbery's naked maze,
Where the vegetable blaze
Of Flora's brightest 'broidery shone,
Every chequer'd charm is flown;
25 Save that the lilac hangs to view
Its bursting gems in clusters blue.
  Scant along the ridgy land
The beans their new-born ranks expand:
The fresh-turn'd soil with tender blades
30 Thinly the sprouting barley shades:
Fringing the forest's devious edge,
Half rob'd appears the hawthorn hedge;
Or to the distant eye displays
Weakly green its budding sprays.
35 The swallow, for a moment seen,
Skims in haste the village green:
From the grey moor, on feeble wing,
The screaming plovers idly spring:
The butterfly, gay-painted soon,
40 Explores awhile the tepid noon;
And fondly trusts its tender dies
To fickle suns, and flattering skies.
  Fraught with a transient, frozen shower,
If a cloud should haply lower,
45 Sailing o'er the landscape dark,
Mute on a sudden is the lark;

20 *Tinctures . . . gale:* perfumes the passing breeze.
21 *naked:* bare of leaves.
24 *chequer'd:* variegated.
31 *devious:* winding.
39 *soon:* early (i.e. in the year).

But when gleams the sun again
O'er the pearl-besprinkled plain,
And from behind his wat'ry vail
50 Looks through the thin-descending hail;
She mounts, and lessening to the sight,
Salutes the blythe return of light,
And high her tuneful track pursues
Mid the dim rainbow's scatter'd hues.
55   Where in venerable rows
Widely waving oaks inclose
The moat of yonder antique hall,
Swarm the rooks with clamorous call;
And to the toils of nature true,
60 Wreath their capacious nests anew.
    Musing through the lawny park,
The lonely poet loves to mark,
How various greens in faint degrees
Tinge the tall groupes of various trees;
65 While, careless of the changing year,
The pine cerulean, never sear,
Towers distinguish'd from the rest,
And proudly vaunts her winter vest.
    Within some whispering osier-ile,
70 Where GLYM's low banks neglected smile;
And each trim meadow still retains
The wintery torrent's oozy stains:
Beneath a willow, long forsook,
The fisher seeks his custom'd nook,
75 And startles from their sedge-wove wood
The bashful wild-duck's early brood.

61 *lawny:* with many glades among the trees.

66 *cerulean:* blue.   *sear:* withered.

68 *vest:* attire, robe.   **69** *osier-ile:* islet overgrown with low willows.

70 GLYM: Warton was rector of Kiddington in Oxfordshire. The parish lies by a stream called the Glym. In the neighbourhood are traces of a Roman encampment (the parish being intersected by Akeman Street), and there are the remains of several earthworks.

O'er the broad downs, a novel race,
Frisk the lambs, with faultering pace,
And with eager bleatings fill
80   The foss that skirts the beacon'd hill.
His free-born vigour yet unbroke
To lordly man's usurping yoke,
The bounding colt forgets to play;
Basking beneath the noontide ray,
85   And stretch'd among the daisies pide
Of a green dingle's sloping side:
While far beneath, where nature spreads
Her boundless length of level meads,
In loose luxuriance taught to stray
90   A thousand tumbling rills inlay
With silver veins the vale, or pass
Redundant through the sparkling grass.
Yet, in these presages rude,
Midst her pensive solitude,
95   Fancy, with prophetic glance,
Sees the teeming months advance;
The field, the forest, green and gay,
The dappled slope, the tedded hay;
Sees the reddening orchard blow,
100   The harvest wave, the vintage flow:
Sees June unfold his glossy robe
Of thousand hues o'er all the globe:
Sees Ceres grasp her crown of corn,
And Plenty load her ample horn.

80 *foss:* a ditch. But it can refer to a Roman road; in this case it would be
Akeman Street.

85 *pide:* i.e. pied, variegated, parti-coloured.

86 *dingle:* wooded dell.

92 *Redundant:* overflowing.

98 *tedded:* spread out for drying.

104 *horn:* the cornucopia, symbol of abundance.

John Cunningham

EVENING

THE following stanzas by John Cunningham (1729-73) make up the third
section of "Day: A Pastoral", which appeared in his *Poems, Chiefly Pastoral*
(1766). Cunningham, who had written plays and been a strolling player,
was a poet of no great distinction, but this pleasant and unforced poem
suggests how liberating for the minor poet was the shift away from porten-
tous meditations and pastoral machinery to the evocation of a mood
through simple but accurate description of the country scene.

XIX

O'er the heath the heifer strays
    Free;—(the furrow'd task is done)
Now the village windows blaze,
    Burnish'd by the setting sun.

XX

5 Now he sets behind the hill,
    Sinking from a golden sky:
Can the pencil's mimic skill,
    Copy the refulgent dye?

XXI

Trudging as the plowmen go,
10   (To the smoking hamlet bound)
Giant-like their shadows grow,
    Lengthen'd o'er the level ground.

XXII

Where the rising forest spreads,
    Shelter, for the lordly dome!
15 To their high-built airy beds,
    See the rooks returning home!

14 *the lordly dome:* any imposing building, but here "lordly" may
suggest the home of the lord of the manor.

XXIII

As the Lark with vary'd tune,
  Carrols to the evening loud;
Mark the mild resplendent moon,
20 Breaking through a parted cloud!

XXIV

Now the hermit Howlet peeps
  From the barn, or twisted brake;
And the blue mist slowly creeps,
  Curling on the silver lake.

XXV

25 As the Trout in speckled pride,
  Playful from its bosom springs;
To the banks, a ruffled tide
  Verges in successive rings.

XXVI

Tripping through the silken grass,
30 O'er the path-divided dale,
Mark the rose-complexion'd lass
  With her well-pois'd milking pail.

XXVII

Linnets with unnumber'd notes,
  And the Cuckow bird with two,
35 Tuning sweet their mellow throats,
  Bid the setting sun adieu.

21 *Howlet:* owl.
22 *brake:* thicket.

Mark Akenside

TO THE EVENING-STAR

THE pompous personal manner of Mark Akenside (1721–70), physician and poet, can be sensed in the orotund blank verse of his most famous poem, *The Pleasures of Imagination* (or, in its revised form, *The Pleasures of the Imagination*), and, despite some passages of eloquent description, many readers will echo Dr. Johnson's verdict: "Sir, I could not read it through." In "To the Evening-Star" (published posthumously in 1772) the verse-form seems to have restrained the poet's rhetoric, and despite some awkwardnesses (such as the changes in the person addressed) which may be attributed to the fact that the poem was not revised for publication, it has a cool and placid elegance of phrasing, suggestive of an evening mood rather than of night-thoughts. Very unusually, the printer of the first edition of *The Poems of Mark Akenside* (1772) used "i" for the first-person pronoun: the capitalis-ation of these pronouns is the only change in the following text.

I

> To-night retir'd the queen of heaven
> With young Endymion stays:
> And now to Hesper is it given
> Awhile to rule the vacant sky,
> 5 Till she shall to her lamp supply
> A stream of brighter rays.

II

> O Hesper, while the starry throng
> With awe thy path surrounds,
> Oh listen to my suppliant song,
> 10 If haply now the vocal sphere
> Can suffer thy delighted ear
> To stoop to mortal sounds.

1 *the queen of heaven:* Cynthia, the moon. Her absence from the sky is attributed to her visits to her earthly lover, the shepherd Endymion.

3 *Hesper:* the Evening-star, the planet Venus.

8 *path:* The planet seems to move against the background of stars.

10 *vocal sphere:* This expression refers to the belief, attributed to

III

So may the bridegroom's genial strain
      Thee still invoke to shine:
15 So may the bride's unmarried train
      To Hymen chaunt their flattering vow,
Still that his lucky torch may glow
      With lustre pure as thine.

IV

Far other vows must I prefer
20   To thy indulgent power.
Alass, but now I paid my tear
      On fair Olympia's virgin tomb:
And lo, from thence, in quest I roam
      Of Philomela's bower.

V

25 Propitious send thy golden ray,
      Thou purest light above:
Let no false flame seduce to stray
      Where gulph or steep lie hid for harm:
But lead where music's healing charm
30   May sooth afflicted love.

Pythagoras, that since the planets moved at different speeds, they must produce different notes which harmonise in the "music of the spheres".

13-14 From Roman times, bridegrooms were described as summoning the Evening-star, the bride was not brought to her husband until evening. *genial:* nuptial.

16 *Hymen:* god of marriage, whose lighted torch signified a happy union. The bridesmaids prayed that the love should stay bright and pure. *flattering vow:* (1) laudatory promise of devotion, and (2) hopeful (i.e. self-flattering) prayers (that they shall find loving husbands).

19 *vows:* prayers.   *prefer:* offer.
20 *indulgent:* ready to answer prayers.   **21** *but now:* just now.
22 *virgin tomb:* (i) the tomb of a virgin and (ii) a new, unstained tomb. "Olympia" is a name Akenside used on several occasions to address a poetic, and perhaps imaginary, mistress.
24 *Philomela:* the nightingale.
27 *false flame: ignis fatuus,* Cf. *The Seasons,* "Autumn", p. 102, l. 71 *n.*

VI

To them, by many a grateful song
  In happier seasons vow'd,
These lawns, Olympia's haunt, belong:
Oft by yon silver stream we walk'd,
35 Or fix'd, while Philomela talk'd,
  Beneath yon copses stood.

VII

Nor seldom, where the beachen boughs
  That roofless tower invade,
We came while her inchanting Muse
40 The radiant moon above us held:
Till by a clamorous owl compell'd
  She fled the solemn shade.

VIII

But hark; I hear her liquid tone.
  Now, Hesper, guide my feet
45 Down the red marle with moss o'ergrown,
Through yon wild thicket next the plain,
Whose hawthorns choke the winding lane
  Which leads to her retreat.

IX

See the green space: on either hand
50 Inlarg'd it spreads around:
See, in the midst she takes her stand,
Where one old oak his awful shade
Extends o'er half the level mead
  Inclos'd in woods profound.

---

31 *To them:* "Them" seems to have no clear referent. Perhaps the editor misread, in the manuscript, "them" for "thee".

39 *Muse:* i.e. the song of the nightingale.

41 *compell'd:* driven.

45 *red marle:* geologically, New Red Sandstone; but, poetically, used for any reddish earth.

X

55   Hark, how through many a melting note
            She now prolongs her lays:
        How sweetly down the void they float!
        The breeze their magic path attends:
        The stars shine out: the forest bends:
60   The wakeful heifers gaze.

XI

        Whoe'er thou art whom chance may bring
            To this sequester'd spot,
        If then the plaintive Syren sing,
        Oh softly tread beneath her bower,
65   And think of heaven's disposing power,
            Of man's uncertain lot.

XII

        Oh think, o'er all this mortal stage,
            What mournful scenes arise:
        What ruin waits on kingly rage:
70   How often virtue dwells with woe:
        How many griefs from knowledge flow:
            How swiftly pleasure flies.

XIII

        O sacred bird, let me at eve,
            Thus wandering all alone,
75   Thy tender counsel oft receive,
        Bear witness to thy pensive airs,
        And pity nature's common cares,
            Till I forget my own.

63 *Syren:* The Sirens were legendary creatures whose song was of irresistible beauty.

65 *disposing:* controlling and ordering. The word, by contrast, helps to revive the original meaning of "lot" ("drawn by chance", and hence "destiny, portion") in the next line.

69 *waits on:* This phrase, which normally means "waits to serve", is here made to suggest "lies in wait for".

77 *nature's common cares:* the troubles common to all human nature.

George Crabbe

from THE VILLAGE

CRABBE'S most fruitful years followed Wordsworth's, for after the appearance of three poems between 1781 and 1785, he published no more until 1807. Yet much in his manner recalls the satirists of the early eighteenth century, and even his attack on the pastoral was a revival of a battle that had long been won. He was not the first to tire of Corydons, or to describe the wretched condition of the poor; but his determination to speak the truth was new in its refusal to replace the pastoral shepherds with a virtuous peasantry. He did not believe that, in general, poverty, sickness and hardship ennoble men: it was because they did the opposite that he so passionately hated them. In his attempts to show how poor and rich alike share "the kindred vices . . . / Of a poor, blind, bewilder'd, erring race", he is sometimes pedestrian and sometimes sermonising, but his passion had at its service a vivid poetic imagination and a finely controlled medium, capable of such brilliant passages as the weed-ridden prospect of the Suffolk coast, which is both a setting and a symbol of his theme, and, moreover, provides an image for his argument that only those who do not look closely can find much to relish in the "sad splendor" of the agricultural scene.

The following passage is the opening of *The Village* (1783).

from BOOK I (lines 1–181)

The village life, and every care that reigns
O'er youthful peasants and declining swains;
What labour yields, and what, that labour past,
Age, in its hour of languor, finds at last;
5   What forms the real picture of the poor,
Demands a song—The Muse can give no more.

Fled are those times, if e'er such times were seen,
When rustic poets prais'd their native green;

1–6 the characteristic manner of opening a poem in the Georgic tradition, though not the characteristic content.
5 *real:* pronounced as a dissyllable.

No shepherds now in smooth alternate verse,
10   Their country's beauty or their nymphs' rehearse;
Yet still for these we frame the tender strain,
Still in our lays fond Corydons complain,
And shepherds' boys their amorous pains reveal,
The only pains, alas! they never feel.

15   On Mincio's banks, in Caesar's bounteous reign,
If TITYRUS found the golden age again,
Must sleepy bards the flattering dream prolong,
Mechanic echos of the Mantuan song?
From truth and nature shall we widely stray,
20   Where VIRGIL, not where fancy leads the way?

Yes, thus the Muses sing of happy swains,
Because the Muses never knew their pains:
They boast their peasants' pipes, but peasants now
Resign their pipes and plod behind the plough;
25   And few amid the rural tribe have time
To number syllables and play with rhyme;
Save honest DUCK, what son of verse could share
The poet's rapture and the peasant's care?
Or the great labours of the field degrade
30   With the new peril of a poorer trade?

From one chief cause these idle praises spring,
That, themes so easy, few forbear to sing;

12 *Corydon:* a shepherd in Virgil's *Eclogues*, who became a type of the love-sick swain. Even Thomson in a youthful poem called "Of a Country Life" speaks of shepherds singing "to soothe their raging amorous pains".

16 TITYRUS: a shepherd in Virgil's *Eclogues*, often identified with Virgil himself, "The Mantuan". Virgil foretold a new Golden Age in the reign of Augustus Caesar. The Mincio is a tributary of the Tiber. Mantua, where Virgil was born, stands on it, and it is mentioned in *Eclogue VII*.

19 *nature:* here, "fundamental human nature", but in line 110, "Nature" means "the natural world".

27 DUCK: Stephen Duck (1705–56), an agricultural labourer, who was lionised for his poetry in the early years of the century, took holy orders, and finally drowned himself in a fit of depression.

They ask no thought, require no deep design,
But swell the song and liquefy the line;
35   The gentle lover takes the rural strain,
A nymph his mistress and himself a swain;
With no sad scenes he clouds his tuneful prayer,
But all, to look like her, is painted fair.

I grant indeed that fields and flocks have charms,
40   For him that gazes or for him that farms;
But when amid such pleasing scenes I trace
The poor laborious natives of the place,
And see the mid-day sun, with fervid ray,
On their bare heads and dewy temples play;
45   While some, with feebler hands and fainter hearts,
Deplore their fortune, yet sustain their parts,
Then shall I dare these real ills to hide,
In tinsel trappings of poetic pride?

No, cast by Fortune on a frowning coast,
50   Which can no groves nor happy vallies boast;
Where other cares than those the Muse relates,
And other shepherds dwell with other mates;
By such examples taught, I paint the cot,
As truth will paint it, and as bards will not:
55   Nor you, ye poor, of letter'd scorn complain,
To you the smoothest song is smooth in vain;
O'ercome by labour and bow'd down by time,
Feel you the barren flattery of a rhyme?
Can poets sooth you, when you pine for bread,
60   By winding myrtles round your ruin'd shed?

34 *liquefy:* make smooth and fluent (because there is no troublesome content).

44 *dewy:* i.e. with sweat.

49 *a frowning coast:* Crabbe was born at Aldeburgh on the Suffolk coast and spent most of his life in the neighbourhood.

51 *Where other cares:* Either *are* has been elided after "where", or the verb "dwell" must go with "cares", as well as with "shepherds" in the next line.

60 *myrtles:* Like laurel, this evergreen was particularly associated with poets. Cf. "Lycidas", l. 2.

Can their light tales your weighty griefs o'erpower,
Or glad with airy mirth the toilsome hour?

Lo! where the heath, with withering brake grown o'er,
Lends the light turf that warms the neighbouring poor;
65 From thence a length of burning sand appears,
Where the thin harvest waves its wither'd ears;
Rank weeds, that every art and care defy,
Reign o'er the land and rob the blighted rye:
There thistles stretch their prickly arms afar,
70 And to the ragged infant threaten war;
There poppies nodding, mock the hope of toil,
There the blue bugloss paints the sterile soil;
Hardy and high, above the slender sheaf,
The slimy mallow waves her silky leaf;
75 O'er the young shoot the charlock throws a shade,
And the wild tare clings round the sickly blade;
With mingled tints the rocky coasts abound,
And a sad splendor vainly shines around.

So looks the nymph whom wretched arts adorn,
80 Betray'd by man, then left for man to scorn;
Whose cheek in vain assumes the mimic rose,
While her sad eyes the troubled breast disclose;
Whose outward splendor is but Folly's dress,
Exposing most, when most it gilds distress.

85   Here joyless roam a wild amphibious race,
With sullen woe display'd in every face;

63 *brake:* here probably means "bracken" rather than "brushwood".

64 *turf:* At this period the poor in country districts were dependent on turf fires.

69–78 Crabbe's eye is picking out the colourful and prolific weeds—purple thistles and mallow, blue bugloss and tares, yellow charlock, scarlet poppies. His references are accurate: mallow plants may grow four feet high and retain moisture on their hairy leaves and stems; the broad-leaved charlock is particularly harmful to young corn; and the common tare, being a kind of vetch, has tendrils which can cling round other plants.

81 *assumes the mimic rose:* is coloured with cosmetics.

85 *amphibious:* The peasants worked the land and fished.

Who, far from civil arts and social fly,
And scowl at strangers with suspicious eye.

Here too the lawless vagrant of the main
90 Draws from his plough th' intoxicated swain;
Want only claim'd the labour of the day,
But vice now steals his nightly rest away.

Where are the swains, who, daily labour done,
With rural games play'd down the setting sun;
95 Who struck with matchless force the bounding ball,
Or made the pond'rous quoit obliquely fall;
While some huge Ajax, terrible and strong,
Engag'd some artful stripling of the throng,
And foil'd beneath the young Ulysses fell;
100 When peals of praise the merry mischief tell?
Where now are these? Beneath yon cliff they stand,
To show the freighted pinnace where to land;
To load the ready steed with guilty haste,
To fly in terror o'er the pathless waste,
105 Or when detected in their straggling course,
To foil their foes by cunning or by force;
Or yielding part (when equal knaves contest)
To gain a lawless passport for the rest.

Here wand'ring long amid these frowning fields,
110 I sought the simple life that Nature yields;

89 *lawless vagrant of the main:* the deep-sea sailor, who, being idle between voyages, would encourage the landworker to waste the day drinking with him.

95 Cricket became extremely popular among all classes during the eighteenth century.

96 *quoit:* a heavy disc of stone or metal hurled like a discus.

97–9 During the funeral games for Patroclus in the *Iliad* Odysseus (Ulysses) wrestles with the heavier Ajax, trips him, and falls on top of him.

98 *artful:* skilful. But in line 112 it seems to have the modern sense of "cunning".

102 *pinnace:* a light sailing-vessel, suitable by speed for smuggling.

107–8 i.e. bribing rascally excisemen.

Rapine and Wrong and Fear usurp'd her place,
And a bold, artful, surly, savage race;
Who, only skill'd to take the finny tribe,
The yearly dinner, or septennial bribe,
115   Wait on the shore, and as the waves run high,
On the tost vessel bend their eager eye;
Which to their coast directs its vent'rous way,
Theirs, or the ocean's miserable prey.

   As on their neighbouring beach yon swallows stand,
120   And wait for favouring winds to leave the land;
While still for flight the ready wing is spread:
So waited I the favouring hour, and fled;
Fled from these shores where guilt and famine reign,
And cry'd, Ah! hapless they who still remain;
125   Who still remain to hear the ocean roar,
Whose greedy waves devour the lessening shore;
Till some fierce tide, with more imperious sway,
Sweeps the low hut and all it holds away;
When the sad tenant weeps from door to door,
130   And begs a poor protection from the poor.

   But these are scenes where Nature's niggard hand
Gave a spare portion to the famish'd land;
Hers is the fault if here mankind complain
Of fruitless toil and labour spent in vain;
135   But yet in other scenes more fair in view,
Where Plenty smiles—alas! she smiles for few,

114 Since 1716, members of Parliament had been elected for seven years; consequently bribes came to voters septennially. The annual dinners were presumably those given by the member to his supporters, but may be a more local form of corruption.

123 *Fled:* Crabbe had temporarily left his native area at the time of writing this poem.

126 *lessening shore:* Aldeburgh's prosperity as a port had been severely diminished by large-scale erosion.

132 *spare:* scanty.

And those who taste not, yet behold her store, ⎫
Are as the slaves that dig the golden ore, ⎬
The wealth around them makes them doubly poor: ⎭
140 Or will you deem them amply paid in health,
Labour's fair child, that languishes with Wealth?
Go then! and see them rising with the sun,
Through a long course of daily toil to run;
Like him to make the plenteous harvest grow,
145 And yet not share the plenty they bestow;
See them beneath the dog-star's raging heat,
When the knees tremble and the temples beat;
Behold them leaning on their scythes, look o'er
The labour past, and toils to come explore;
150 See them alternate suns and showers engage,
And hoard up aches and anguish for their age;
Thro' fens and marshy moors their steps pursue,
When their warm pores imbibe the evening dew;
Then own that labour may as fatal be
155 To these thy slaves, as luxury to thee.

Amid this tribe too oft a manly pride
Strives in strong toil the fainting heart to hide;
There may you see the youth of slender frame
Contend with weakness, weariness, and shame;
160 Yet urged along, and proudly loth to yield,
He strives to join his fellows of the field;
Till long contending nature droops at last,
Declining health rejects his poor repast,
His cheerless spouse the coming danger sees,
165 And mutual murmurs urge the slow disease.

Yet grant them health, 'tis not for us to tell,
Though the head droops not, that the heart is well;

---

146 *the dog-star's raging heat:* The dog-days from early July to mid-August were supposed to be particularly hot because Sirius, the dog-star, rose with the sun and added its own heat.

165 *mutual murmurs:* grumbles about each other.   *urge:* hasten.

Or will you urge their homely, plenteous fare,
Healthy and plain and still the poor man's share?
170 Oh! trifle not with wants you cannot feel,
Nor mock the misery of a stinted meal;
Homely not wholesome, plain not plenteous, such
As you who envy would disdain to touch.

Ye gentle souls who dream of rural ease,
175 Whom the smooth stream and smoother sonnet please;
Go! if the peaceful cot your praises share,
Go look within, and ask if peace be there:
If peace be his—that drooping weary sire,
Or theirs, that offspring round their feeble fire,
180 Or hers, that matron pale, whose trembling hand
Turns on the wretched hearth th' expiring brand.

175 *sonnet:* any lyric poem.

William Blake

TO THE EVENING STAR

EVEN in this early poem the intensity of Blake's poetic imagination transforms the traditional address. Blake is clearly not speaking to the planet Venus or to some mythological goddess; he is even more clearly not concerned with the threat to English sheep from lions and wolves. The star might be said to symbolise some beneficent spirit as the sheep symbolise mankind, and the beasts of prey what the Prayer-book calls "all perils and dangers of this night". But Blake would not have welcomed a crude reduction of his poetic vision to allegory: "Vision or imagination is a representation of what eternally exists, really and unchangeably." He called the star an "angel" not as a poetic fancy but because he saw it that way.

"What," it will be question'd, "when the sun rises, do you not see a round disk of fire somewhat like a guinea?" O no, no, I see an innumerable company of the heavenly host crying "Holy, Holy, Holy is the Lord God Almighty". I question not my corporeal or vegetative eye any more than I would question a window concerning a sight. I look thro' it and not with it.

The text is from *Poetical Sketches* (1783). The above quotations are from *A Vision of the Last Judgment*.

> Thou fair-hair'd angel of the evening,
> Now, whilst the sun rests on the mountains, light
> Thy bright torch of love; thy radiant crown
> Put on, and smile upon our evening bed!
> 5   Smile on our loves; and, while thou drawest the
> Blue curtains of the sky, scatter thy silver dew
> On every flower that shuts its sweet eyes
> In timely sleep. Let thy west wind sleep on
> The lake; speak silence with thy glimmering eyes,
> 10   And wash the dusk with silver. Soon, full soon,
> Dost thou withdraw; then the wolf rages wide,
> And the lion glares thro' the dun forest:
> The fleeces of our flocks are cover'd with
> Thy sacred dew: protect them with thine influence.

12 *dun:* In poetry the word often means "dark" or "murky".

William Cowper

from THE TASK

The Task (1785) has to be represented by extracts, since the smallest of its books is nearly 800 lines long, but extracts are less damaging to Cowper's poem than to, say, *The Seasons*. Lady Austen's suggestion, when the poet was recovering from one of his recurring mental breakdowns, that he should occupy his mind by writing a blank-verse poem about the sofa on which he was convalescing, set him off on a long wandering work, guided by random reflections and associations to such an extent that the one difficulty about calling it digressive is that there is no central matter from which to digress. As a consequence of this method, if it can be called a method, and of Cowper's remarkable facility, he produced a great but unequal poem, where beautifully accurate and evocative writing is interspersed with passages of rather pedestrian verse. Yet whenever he moves to a subject which excites his imagination (especially when he is describing the

countryside and countrymen he knew), he finds a true personal eloquence.
His ear for sounds and rhythms is as sharp as Thomson's—the lines about
the waggoner in the storm lumber and strain onwards, the description of
the dog in the snow moves in sudden bounds and halts—and he responds to
the beauty of ordinary things, like daily work skilfully done. He is less
scientific and dramatic than Thomson, less spiritually and morally elevated
than Wordsworth: his gift is for the intimate understanding and detailed
perception of what is familiar, so that he illustrates his own assertion that
"Scenes must be beautiful which daily view'd / Please daily".

The text is that of the first edition of 1785.

I

from BOOK ONE. THE SOFA (lines 154–366)

How oft upon yon eminence, our pace
Has slacken'd to a pause, and we have borne
The ruffling wind scarce conscious that it blew,
While admiration feeding at the eye,
5   And still unsated, dwelt upon the scene.
Thence with what pleasure have we just discern'd
The distant plough slow-moving, and beside
His lab'ring team that swerv'd not from the track,
The sturdy swain diminish'd to a boy!
10   Here Ouse, slow winding through a level plain
Of spacious meads with cattle sprinkled o'er,
Conducts the eye along his sinuous course
Delighted. There, fast rooted in his bank
Stand, never overlook'd, our fav'rite elms
15   That screen the herdsman's solitary hut;
While far beyond and overthwart the stream
That as with molten glass inlays the vale,
The sloping land recedes into the clouds;

1 *our pace:* The partner of Cowper's walks was Mary Unwin. This
particular walk was from Olney in Buckinghamshire, where the poet
lived, to Weston, and, in particular, to a hill, known as "The Cliff", in
the grounds of Weston House.

4 *admiration:* wonder.

Displaying on its varied side, the grace
20 Of hedge-row beauties numberless, square tow'r,
Tall spire, from which the sound of chearful bells
Just undulates upon the list'ning ear;
Groves, heaths, and smoking villages remote.
Scenes must be beautiful which daily view'd
25 Please daily, and whose novelty survives
Long knowledge and the scrutiny of years.
Praise justly due to those that I describe.

Nor rural sights alone, but rural sounds
Exhilarate the spirit, and restore
30 The tone of languid Nature. Mighty winds
That sweep the skirt of some far-spreading wood
Of ancient growth, make music not unlike
The dash of ocean on his winding shore,
And lull the spirit while they fill the mind,
35 Unnumber'd branches waving in the blast,
And all their leaves fast flutt'ring, all at once.
Nor less composure waits upon the roar
Of distant floods, or on the softer voice
Of neighb'ring fountain, or of rills that slip
40 Through the cleft rock, and chiming as they fall
Upon loose pebbles, lose themselves at length
In matted grass, that with a livelier green
Betrays the secret of their silent course.
Nature inanimate employs sweet sounds,
45 But animated Nature sweeter still
To sooth and satisfy the human ear.
Ten thousand warblers chear the day, and one
The live-long night: nor these alone whose notes
Nice-finger'd art must emulate in vain,

20–3 As evidence of the exactness Cowper aimed at, it may be noticed that contemporaries identified all the places mentioned in the poem. The "square tow'r" was that of Clifton Reynes church, the "tall spire" Olney church, and the "villages", Steventon and Emberton.

49 *Nice-finger'd:* capable of delicate (but perhaps over-refined) touches. Music, of course, is the art Cowper has particularly in mind.

50   But cawing rooks, and kites that swim sublime
      In still repeated circles, screaming loud,
      The jay, the pie, and ev'n the boding owl
      That hails the rising moon, have charms for me.
      Sounds inharmonious in themselves and harsh,
55   Yet heard in scenes where peace for ever reigns,
      And only there, please highly for their sake.

      Peace to the artist, whose ingenious thought
      Devised the weather-house, that useful toy!
      Fearless of humid air and gathering rains
60   Forth steps the man, an emblem of myself,
      More delicate his tim'rous mate retires.
      When Winter soaks the fields, and female feet
      Too weak to struggle with tenacious clay,
      Or ford the rivulets, are best at home,
65   The task of new discov'ries falls on me.
      At such a season and with such a charge
      Once went I forth, and found, till then unknown,
      A cottage, whither oft we since repair:
      'Tis perch'd upon the green-hill top, but close
70   Inviron'd with a ring of branching elms
      That overhang the thatch, itself unseen,
      Peeps at the vale below; so thick beset
      With foliage of such dark redundant growth,
      I call'd the low-roof'd lodge the *peasant's nest.*
75   And hidden as it is, and far remote
      From such unpleasing sounds as haunt the ear
      In village or in town, the bay of curs
      Incessant, clinking hammers, grinding wheels,
      And infants clam'rous whether pleas'd or pain'd,
80   Oft have I wish'd the peaceful covert mine.
      Here, I have said, at least I should possess
      The poet's treasure, silence, and indulge

52 *pie:* magpie.

58 *weather-house:* once a familiar household ornament. From a small wooden house a man emerged when the air was damp and a woman when it was dry.   **80** *covert:* shelter.

The dreams of fancy, tranquil and secure.
Vain thought! the dweller in that still retreat
85 Dearly obtains the refuge it affords.
Its elevated scite forbids the wretch
To drink sweet waters of the chrystal well;
He dips his bowl into the weedy ditch,
And heavy-laden brings his bev'rage home
90 Far-fetch'd and little worth; nor seldom waits,
Dependent on the baker's punctual call,
To hear his creaking panniers at the door,
Angry and sad and his last crust consumed.
So farewel envy of the *peasant's nest.*
95 If solitude make scant the means of life,
Society for me! thou seeming sweet,
Be still a pleasing object in my view,
My visit still, but never mine abode.

Not distant far, a length of colonade
100 Invites us. Monument of ancient taste,
Now scorn'd, but worthy of a better fate.
Our fathers knew the value of a screen
From sultry suns, and in their shaded walks
And long-protracted bow'rs, enjoy'd at noon
105 The gloom and coolness of declining day.
We bear our shades about us; self depriv'd
Of other screen, the thin umbrella spread,
And range an Indian waste without a tree.
Thanks to Benevolus—he spares me yet
110 These chesnuts ranged in corresponding lines,
And though himself so polish'd, still reprieves
The obsolete prolixity of shade.

86 *scite:* site, situation.
99 *colonade:* an avenue of (chestnut) trees, leading to the Rustic Bridge.
109 *Benevolus:* "John Courtney Throckmorton, Esq., of Weston Underwood." (*Cowper, 1785.*)
112 *The obsolete prolixity of shade:* Cowper is fond of polysyllabic humour. His point is that the umbrella has made the shade of the trees both out of date and superfluous; but he does not share the taste of his times.

Descending now (but cautious, lest too fast)
A sudden steep, upon a rustic bridge
115 We pass a gulph in which the willows dip
Their pendent boughs, stooping as if to drink.
Hence ancle deep in moss and flow'ry thyme
We mount again, and feel at ev'ry step
Our foot half sunk in hillocks green and soft,
120 Rais'd by the mole, the miner of the soil.
He not unlike the great ones of mankind,
Disfigures earth, and plotting in the dark
Toils much to earn a monumental pile,
That may record the mischiefs he has done.

125 The summit gain'd, behold the proud alcove
That crowns it! yet not all its pride secures
The grand retreat from injuries impress'd
By rural carvers, who with knives deface
The pannels, leaving an obscure rude name
130 In characters uncouth, and spelt amiss.
So strong the zeal t' immortalize himself
Beats in the breast of man, that ev'n a few
Few transient years won from th' abyss abhorr'd
Of blank oblivion, seem a glorious prize,
135 And even to a clown. Now roves the eye,
And posted on this speculative height
Exults in its command. The sheep-fold here
Pours out its fleecy tenants o'er the glebe.
At first, progressive as a stream, they seek
140 The middle field; but scatter'd by degrees
Each to his choice, soon whiten all the land.
There from the sun-burnt hay-field homeward creeps
The loaded wain, while lighten'd of its charge

125 *alcove:* a kind of summer-house with six panelled sides, three of
which were left open to the view.
136 *speculative:* commanding a wide prospect.
138 *glebe:* here, "field".
139 *progressive:* moving forward as though in procession.
140 *The middle field:* the middle of the field.

The wain that meets it, passes swiftly by,
145   The boorish driver leaning o'er his team
Vocif'rous, and impatient of delay.
Nor less attractive is the woodland scene
Diversified with trees of ev'ry growth
Alike yet various. Here the grey smooth trunks
150   Of ash or lime, or beech, distinctly shine,
Within the twilight of their distant shades;
There lost behind a rising ground, the wood
Seems sunk, and shorten'd to its topmost boughs.
No tree in all the grove but has its charms,
155   Though each its hue peculiar; paler some,
And of a wannish grey; the willow such
And poplar, that with silver lines his leaf,
And ash far-stretching his umbrageous arm.
Of deeper green the elm; and deeper still,
160   Lord of the woods, the long-surviving oak.
Some glossy-leav'd and shining in the sun,
The maple, and the beech of oily nuts
Prolific, and the lime at dewy eve
Diffusing odors: nor unnoted pass
165   The sycamore, capricious in attire,
Now green, now tawny, and, 'ere autumn yet
Have changed the woods, in scarlet honors bright.
O'er these, but far beyond, (a spacious map
Of hill and valley interpos'd between)
170   The Ouse, dividing the well water'd land,
Now glitters in the sun, and now retires,
As bashful, yet impatient to be seen.

Hence the declivity is sharp and short,
And such the re-ascent; between them weeps
175   A little Naiad her impov'rish'd urn
All summer long, which winter fills again.

150 *distinctly:* individually. **167** *honors:* See *Windsor-Forest*, p. 52, l. 219 *n*.
175 *A little Naiad:* a personification of a little channel cut to drain a
hollow. In summer it was dry. Naiads were nymphs of sources and streams,
and were generally represented holding urns from which water flowed.

The folded gates would bar my progress now,
But that the Lord of this inclosed demesne,
Communicative of the good he owns,
180 Admits me to a share: the guiltless eye
Commits no wrong, nor wastes what it enjoys.
Refreshing change! where now the blazing sun?
By short transition we have lost his glare
And stepp'd at once into a cooler clime.
185 Ye fallen avenues! once more I mourn
Your fate unmerited, once more rejoice
That yet a remnant of your race survives.
How airy and how light the graceful arch,
Yet awful as the consecrated roof
190 Re-echoing pious anthems! while beneath
The chequer'd earth seems restless as a flood
Brush'd by the wind. So sportive is the light
Shot through the boughs, it dances as they dance,
Shadow and sunshine intermingling quick,
195 And darkning and enlightning, as the leaves
Play wanton, ev'ry moment, ev'ry spot.

    And now with nerves new-brac'd and spirits chear'd
We tread the wilderness, whose well-roll'd walks
With curvature of slow and easy sweep,
200 Deception innocent—give ample space
To narrow bounds. The grove receives us next;
Between the upright shafts of whose tall elms
We may discern the thresher at his task.
Thump after thump, resounds the constant flail,
205 That seems to swing uncertain, and yet falls
Full on the destin'd ear. Wide flies the chaff,
The rustling straw sends up a frequent mist
Of atoms sparkling in the noon-day beam.

177 *folded:* closed.
178 *the Lord:* "See the foregoing note" (*Cowper, 1785*): i.e. note on
l. 109. Throckmorton allowed Cowper to keep a key to his park.
196 *Play wanton:* twist and turn in a fickle way.
198 *wilderness:* See *A Country Walk*, p. 97, l. 116 *n*.

Come hither, ye that press your beds of down
210   And sleep not: see him sweating o'er his bread
Before he eats it.—'Tis the primal curse,
But soften'd into mercy; made the pledge
Of chearful days, and nights without a groan.

211 *the primal curse:* that Adam and his descendants should eat their bread in the sweat of their faces (*Genesis*, iii, 19).

II

from BOOK IV. THE WINTER EVENING
(lines 1–87)

Hark! 'tis the twanging horn! o'er yonder bridge
That with its wearisome but needful length
Bestrides the wintry flood, in which the moon
Sees her unwrinkled face reflected bright,
5   He comes, the herald of a noisy world,
With spatter'd boots, strapp'd waist, and frozen locks,
News from all nations lumb'ring at his back.
True to his charge the close-pack'd load behind,
Yet careless what he brings, his one concern
10   Is to conduct it to the destin'd inn,
And having dropp'd th' expected bag—pass on.
He whistles as he goes, light-hearted wretch,
Cold and yet cheerful: messenger of grief
Perhaps to thousands, and of joy to some,
15   To him indiff'rent whether grief or joy.
Houses in ashes, and the fall of stocks,
Births, deaths, and marriages, epistles wet
With tears that trickled down the writers' cheeks

1 *horn:* The post-boy, travelling on horseback, announced his approach by blowing his horn. In his pack he carried the London newspapers as well as the mail.

2 *needful length:* A wooden bridge stretched across the valley between Olney and Emberton. It was necessarily long because in winter the valley was often flooded.

Fast as the periods from his fluent quill,
20 Or charged with am'rous sighs of absent swains
Or nymphs responsive, equally affect
His horse and him, unconscious of them all.
But oh th' important budget! usher'd in
With such heart-shaking music, who can say
25 What are its tidings? have our troops awaked?
Or do they still, as if with opium drugg'd,
Snore to the murmurs of th' Atlantic wave?
Is India free? and does she wear her plumed
And jewelled turban with a smile of peace,
30 Or do we grind her still? the grand debate,
The popular harangue, the tart reply,
The logic and the wisdom and the wit
And the loud laugh—I long to know them all;
I burn to set th' imprison'd wranglers free,
35 And give them voice and utt'rance once again.

Now stir the fire, and close the shutters fast,
Let fall the curtains, wheel the sofa round,
And while the bubbling and loud-hissing urn
Throws up a steamy column, and the cups
40 That cheer but not inebriate, wait on each,
So let us welcome peaceful evening in.
Not such his evening, who with shining face

19 *periods:* sentences.

21 *responsive:* replying to their admirers' letters.

23 *budget:* strictly "a wallet or pouch": but here the word means "a journal".

25–30 While Cowper was writing this poem (from the summer of 1783 to the late summer of 1784) Britain was being forced to agree to peace-terms after the defeat of her armies in the American War of Independence, and there was great concern over the conduct of Indian affairs, which led, a few years later, to the impeachment of Warren Hastings. A war in Mysore was concluded in March 1784.

39–40 *the cups that cheer but not inebriate:* i.e. tea. Cowper is jokingly recalling the application of this expression to tar-water by Bishop Berkeley in *Siris* (1747).

Sweats in the crowded theatre, and, squeezed
And bored with elbow-points through both his sides,
45   Out scolds the ranting actor on the stage.
Nor his, who patient stands 'till his feet throb
And his head thumps, to feed upon the breath
Of patriots bursting with heroic rage,
Or placemen, all tranquillity and smiles.
50   This folio of four pages, happy work!
Which not ev'n critics criticise, that holds
Inquisitive attention while I read
Fast bound in chains of silence, which the fair,
Though eloquent themselves, yet fear to break,
55   What is it but a map of busy life
Its fluctuations and its vast concerns?
Here runs the mountainous and craggy ridge
That tempts ambition. On the summit, see,
The seals of office glitter in his eyes;
60   He climbs, he pants, he grasps them. At his heels,
Close at his heels a demagogue ascends,
And with a dext'rous jerk soon twists him down
And wins them, but to lose them in his turn.
Here rills of oily eloquence in soft
65   Mæanders lubricate the course they take;
The modest speaker is ashamed and grieved
T' engross a moment's notice, and yet begs,
Begs a propitious ear for his poor thoughts,
However trivial all that he conceives.
70   Sweet bashfulness! it claims, at least, this praise,
The dearth of information and good sense
That it foretells us, always comes to pass.
Cataracts of declamation thunder here,
There forests of no-meaning spread the page
75   In which all comprehension wanders lost;
While fields of pleasantry amuse us there,
With merry descants on a nation's woes.
The rest appears a wilderness of strange

49 *placemen:* men who, through influence, have obtained governmental positions.   **50** *folio:* the newspaper, later described in terms of a landscape.

But gay confusion, roses for the cheeks
80 And lilies for the brows of faded age,
Teeth for the toothless, ringlets for the bald,
Heav'n, earth, and ocean plunder'd of their sweets,
Nectareous essences, Olympian dews,
Sermons and city feasts and fav'rite airs,
85 Ætherial journies, submarine exploits,
And Katterfelto with his hair on end
At his own wonders, wond'ring for his bread.

79 *gay confusion:* the advertisements and news-snippets which Cowper enumerates.

83 *Nectareous ... dews:* Advertisers' language was as extravagant in Cowper's time as in ours. Nectar was the drink of the gods, and Olympus their home. **84** *airs:* tunes.

85 *Ætherial journies, submarine exploits:* The year 1783 when Cowper began his poem was the year of the first successful launching of a balloon (June), the first manned ascent (October), the first free flight (November), and the first ascent in England (November). Cowper, like everyone else, was stirred: his letters at the time were full of references to the flights and he attended an unsuccessful attempt by his neighbour Throckmorton to launch a balloon. Submarines, too, were very much in the news, following the success in 1775 of an American model propelled by hand.

86 *Katterfelto:* a quack who died in 1799. His advertisements began "Wonders! Wonders! Wonders!"

III

from BOOK IV. THE WINTER EVENING
(lines 243–373)

Come evening once again, season of peace,
Return sweet evening, and continue long!
Methinks I see thee in the streaky west,
With matron-step slow-moving, while the night
5 Treads on thy sweeping train; one hand employ'd
In letting fall the curtain of repose
On bird and beast, the other charged for man
With sweet oblivion of the cares of day;
Not sumptuously adorn'd, nor needing aid

10 Like homely featur'd night, of clust'ring gems,
    A star or two just twinkling on thy brow
    Suffices thee; save that the moon is thine
    No less than hers, not worn indeed on high
    With ostentatious pageantry, but set
15 With modest grandeur in thy purple zone,
    Resplendent less, but of an ampler round.
    Come then, and thou shalt find thy vot'ry calm
    Or make me so. Composure is thy gift.
    And whether I devote thy gentle hours
20 To books, to music, or the poet's toil,
    To weaving nets for bird-alluring fruit;
    Or twining silken threads round iv'ry reels
    When they command whom man was born to please,
    I slight thee not, but make thee welcome still.

25   Just when our drawing-rooms begin to blaze
    With lights by clear reflection multiplied
    From many a mirrour, in which he of Gath
    Goliah, might have seen his giant bulk
    Whole without stooping, tow'ring crest and all,
30 My pleasures too begin. But me perhaps
    The glowing hearth may satisfy awhile
    With faint illumination that uplifts
    The shadow to the cieling, there by fits
    Dancing uncouthly to the quiv'ring flame.
35 Not undelightful is an hour to me
    So spent in parlour twilight; such a gloom
    Suits well the thoughtfull or unthinking mind,
    The mind contemplative, with some new theme
    Pregnant, or indisposed alike to all.
40 Laugh ye, who boast your more mercurial pow'rs
    That never feel a stupor, know no pause
    Nor need one. I am conscious, and confess
    Fearless, a soul that does not always think.

15 *zone:* girdle.   **21** *nets:* to spread over fruit-bushes.
28 *Goliah:* the giant of Gath (*First Book of Samuel*, xvii).
34 *uncouthly:* grotesquely.

Me oft has fancy ludicrous and wild
45 Sooth'd with a waking dream of houses, tow'rs,
Trees, churches, and strange visages express'd
In the red cinders, while with poring eye
I gazed, myself creating what I saw.
Nor less amused have I quiescent watch'd
50 The sooty films that play upon the bars
Pendulous, and foreboding in the view
Of superstition prophesying still
Though still deceived, some stranger's near approach.
'Tis thus the understanding takes repose
55 In indolent vacuity of thought,
And sleeps and is refresh'd. Meanwhile the face
Conceals the mood lethargic with a mask
Of deep deliberation, as the man
Were task'd to his full strength, absorb'd and lost.
60 Thus oft reclin'd at ease, I lose an hour
At evening, till at length the freezing blast
That sweeps the bolted shutter, summons home
The recollected powers, and snapping short
The glassy threads with which the fancy weaves
65 Her brittle toys, restores me to myself.
How calm is my recess, and how the frost
Raging abroad, and the rough wind, endear
The silence and the warmth enjoy'd within.
I saw the woods and fields at close of day
70 A variegated show; the meadows green
Though faded, and the lands where lately waved
The golden harvest, of a mellow brown,
Upturn'd so lately by the forceful share.
I saw far off the weedy fallows smile
75 With verdure not unprofitable, grazed
By flocks fast feeding and selecting each
His fav'rite herb; while all the leafless groves
That skirt th' horizon wore a sable hue,

49 ff. Cf. "Frost at Midnight", p. 183, ll. 15 ff. and note.
64–5 *The glassy threads . . . toys:* Cowper is probably thinking of small trinkets made of glass filaments.

Scarce noticed in the kindred dusk of eve.
80 To-morrow brings a change, a total change!
Which even now, though silently perform'd
And slowly, and by most unfelt, the face
Of universal nature undergoes.
Fast falls a fleecy show'r. The downy flakes
85 Descending and with never-ceasing lapse
Softly alighting upon all below,
Assimilate all objects. Earth receives
Gladly the thick'ning mantle, and the green
And tender blade that fear'd the chilling blast,
90 Escapes unhurt beneath so warm a veil.

In such a world, so thorny, and where none
Finds happiness unblighted, or if found,
Without some thistly sorrow at its side,
It seems the part of wisdom, and no sin
95 Against the law of love, to measure lots
With less distinguish'd than ourselves, that thus
We may with patience bear our mod'rate ills,
And sympathise with others, suff'ring more.
Ill fares the trav'ler now, and he that stalks
100 In pond'rous boots beside his reeking team.
The wain goes heavily, impeded sore
By congregated loads adhering close
To the clogg'd wheels; and in its sluggish pace
Noiseless, appears a moving hill of snow.
105 The toiling steeds expand the nostril wide,
While ev'ry breath by respiration strong
Forced downward, is consolidated soon
Upon their jutting chests. He, form'd to bear
The pelting brunt of the tempestuous night,
110 With half-shut eyes and pucker'd cheeks, and teeth
Presented bare against the storm, plods on.
One hand secures his hat, save when with both
He brandishes his pliant length of whip,

100 *reeking:* smoking (i.e. steaming).
107 *consolidated:* frozen.

Resounding oft, and never heard in vain.
115 Oh happy! and in my account, denied
That sensibility of pain with which
Refinement is endued, thrice happy thou.
Thy frame robust and hardy, feels indeed
The piercing cold, but feels it unimpair'd.
120 The learned finger never need explore
Thy vig'rous pulse, and the unhealthful East,
That breathes the spleen, and searches ev'ry bone
Of the infirm, is wholesome air to thee.
Thy days roll on exempt from household care,
125 The waggon is thy wife; and the poor beasts
That drag the dull companion to and fro,
Thine helpless charge, dependent on thy care.
Ah treat them kindly! rude as thou appear'st
Yet show that thou hast mercy, which the great
130 With needless hurry whirl'd from place to place,
Humane as they would seem, not always show.

115 *in my account:* according to my notion.
122 *spleen:* gloomy dejection of spirits or irritability.

IV

from BOOK V. THE WINTER MORNING WALK
(lines 1–51)

'Tis morning; and the sun with ruddy orb
Ascending fires the horizon. While the clouds,
That crowd away before the driving wind,
More ardent as the disk emerges more,
5 Resemble most some city in a blaze,
Seen through the leafless wood. His slanting ray
Slides ineffectual down the snowy vale,
And tinging all with his own rosy hue,

4 *ardent:* burning, or, rather, appearing to be aflame.

From ev'ry herb and ev'ry spiry blade
10 Stretches a length of shadow o'er the field.
Mine, spindling into longitude immense,
In spite of gravity and sage remark
That I myself am but a fleeting shade,
Provokes me to a smile. With eye askance
15 I view the muscular proportioned limb
Transformed to a lean shank. The shapeless pair
As they designed to mock me, at my side
Take step for step, and as I near approach
The cottage, walk along the plaister'd wall
20 Prepost'rous sight! the legs without the man.
The verdure of the plain lies buried deep
Beneath the dazzling deluge, and the bents
And coarser grass upspearing o'er the rest,
Of late unsightly and unseen, now shine
25 Conspicuous, and, in bright apparel clad
And fledged with icy feathers, nod superb.
The cattle mourn in corners where the fence
Screens them, and seem half petrified to sleep
In unrecumbent sadness. There they wait
30 Their wonted fodder, not like hungr'ing man,
Fretfull if unsupplied, but silent, meek,
And patient of the slow-paced swain's delay.
He from the stack carves out th' accustomed load,
Deep-plunging and again deep plunging oft
35 His broad keen knife into the solid mass.
Smooth as a wall the upright remnant stands,
With such undeviating and even force
He severs it away. No needless care,
Lest storms should overset the leaning pile
40 Deciduous, or its own unbalanced weight.
Forth goes the woodman leaving unconcerned
The cheerfull haunts of man, to wield the axe
And drive the wedge in yonder forest drear,
From morn to eve his solitary task.

17 *As:* as if.   **22** *bents:* reedy grasses.
40 *deciduous:* declining, ready to fall.

45 Shaggy and lean and shrew'd, with pointed ears
    And tail cropp'd short, half lurcher and half cur
    His dog attends him. Close behind his heel
    Now creeps he slow, and now with many a frisk
    Wide-scampering snatches up the drifted snow
50 With iv'ry teeth, or ploughs it with his snout;
    Then shakes his powder'd coat and barks for joy.

45 *shrew'd:* mischievous.
46 *lurcher:* a dog cross-bred between the collie and the greyhound.

James Hurdis

from THE VILLAGE CURATE

To produce some kind of blank verse about nature demanded little in powers of mind or skill in versification, and the late eighteenth century overflowed with such verse, much of it uniformly dull and lifeless. A few of the versifiers were, at times, capable of rising above their limitations, and of these Cowper's friend, James Hurdis (1763–1801), is representative. He is saved from dullness by deliberate unpretentiousness: in his best-known poem, *The Village Curate* (1788), he declared his wish to celebrate ordinary vegetables—"the martial pea", "the gay bean", "soporific lettuce", cucumbers:

> All these and more,
> As carrots, parsnips, onions, cabbages,
> Potatoes, turnips, radishes, my Muse
> Disdains not.

He writes diffusely but, apart from religious moralisings, with an unaffected plainness which sometimes produces effects of unconscious humour, and sometimes a little original flavour, as when he anticipates G. K. Chesterton's observation that "the rolling English drunkard made the rolling English road". In the following passage the wandering curate has passed into a thick wood.

> So have I gone at night,
> When the faint eye of day was hardly clos'd,

1 *So have I gone at night:* Hurdis has been describing the dark interior of a wood.

And turn'd the grating key that kept the door
Of church or chapel, to enjoy alone
5 The mournful horrors that impending night
And painted windows shed, along the dark
And scarce to be distinguish'd aisle. My foot
Has stood and paus'd, half startled at the sound
Of its own tip-toe pace. I've held my breath
10 And been offended that my nimble heart
Should throb so audibly. I would not hear
Aught else disturb the silent reign of death,
Save the dull ticking of a restless clock.
That calls me home, and leads the thoughtful soul
15 Thro' mazes of reflection, till she feels
For what and whom she lives. Ye timid fair,
I never saw the sheeted ghost steal by,
I never heard th' unprison'd dead complain
And gibber in my ear, tho' I have lov'd
20 The yawning time of night, and travel'd round
And round again the mansions of the dead.
Yet I have heard, what fancy well might deem
Sufficient proof of both, the prowling owl
Sweep by, and with a hideous shriek awake
25 The church-yard echo, and I too have stood
Harrow'd and speechless at the dismal sound.
But here she frights us not. Such scenes as these
No ghost frequents. If any spirits here,
They are as gentle as the eve of day,
30 And only come to turn our wand'ring steps
From lurking danger. With what easy grace
This footway winds about. Shew me designs
That please us more. What strict geometer
Can carve his yew, his quickset, or his box,
35 To half its elegance? I would not see
A thousand paces on, nor have my way
Too strictly serpentine. If there be art,
Let it be hid in nature. Wind the path,

---

18 *unprison'd:* escaped from their prison.

But be not bound to follow Hogarth's line.
40 I grant it beauty, but too often seen,
That beauty pleases not. I love to meet
A sudden turn like this, that stops me short,
Extravagantly devious, and invites
Or up the hill or down; then winds again,
45 By reeling drunkard trod, and all at once
Ends in a green-sward waggon way, that like
Cathedral aisle compleatly roof'd with branches,
Runs thro' the gloomy wood from top to bottom,
And has at either end a gothic door
50 Wide open. Yet we tarry not, nor tread
With hardly sensible advance the way
That mocks our toil; but having gaz'd awhile
At the still view below, the living scene
Inimitable nature has hung up
55 At the vault's end, we disappear again,
And follow still the flexile path, conceal'd
In shady underwood. Nor sometimes scorn
Under the high majestic oak to sit,
And comment on his leaf, his branch, his arm
60 Paternally extended, his vast girth,
And ample hoop above. To him that loves
To walk with contemplation, ev'ry leaf
Affords a tale concluding with a moral.
The very hazel has a tongue to teach,
65 The birch, the maple, horn-beam, becch, and ash.

39 *Hogarth's line:* In *The Analysis of Beauty* (1753) Hogarth declared that, although all waving lines were ornamental when properly used "yet, strictly speaking, there is but one precise line, properly to be called the line of *beauty*." He attempted to describe this in words and illustrations; in effect, it would seem to be a line moving from smaller to greater reverse curvature, like a drawn-out S.

43 *extravagantly:* in a wandering and irregular way.

56 *flexile:* easily bending.

Robert Fergusson

"NOW MURKY SHADES SURROUND THE POLE"

THIS little night-piece is not representative of the robust but sensitive poetry which Fergusson wrote in Scots, but it is superior to most of his poetry in English because of the simplicity and directness with which it creates a universal image of night.

It appears to have been first published in Arthur Masson's *A Collection of English Prose and Verse, for the Use of Schools . . . The tenth edition, with valuable additions* (1788).

> Now murky shades surround the pole;
> Darkness lords without controul;
> To the notes of buzzing owl
> Lions roar, and tygers howl.
> 5 Fright'ning from their azure shrine,
> Stars that wont in orbs to shine:
> Now the sailors' storm tost bark
> Knows no blest celestial mark,
> While, in the briny troubled deep,
> 10 Dolphins change their sport for sleep:
> Ghosts and frightful spectres gaunt
> Church-yards dreary footsteps haunt,
> And brush, with wither'd arms, the dews
> That fall upon the drooping yews.

1 *pole:* often in poetry means "sky".

2 *without controul:* without restraint or limit.

3 *buzzing:* (1) flying busily about, or (2) muttering, full of busy chatter.

6 *wont:* are wont.

8 *mark:* a star used as guide by steersman.

11–12 *Church-yards* should probably have a possessive apostrophe, *footsteps* then being the stone steps in churchyards. Alternatively the verb *haunt* must be taken with line 11 as well as with line 12.

Robert Burns

TAM O' SHANTER, A TALE

THE connection between "Tam o' Shanter" and earlier night-pieces may seem a tenuous one, but both by its origin and its character the poem is related to the tradition. The fascination with ruins, darkness, and Gothic horrors was closely associated with the growing antiquarian interests of the late eighteenth century, and "Tam o' Shanter" first appeared as a lengthy footnote in the second of the two volumes of Francis Grose's *Antiquities of Scotland* (1789/91). At Burns's suggestion Grose included an engraving of the ruins of Alloa (or Alloway) church, and asked for a poem to face the picture. Burns supplied one which retained much of the nocturnal's characteristics—the midnight hour, the mysteriously illuminated ruins, the stormy night, the owls, corpses, ghosts and spirits—and interspersed mock-serious meditations which in one place lead out of broad Scots into sober English diction and imagery. But he added a humorous realism from folk-tales (like those which, according to Blair, were told "at Wake or Gossiping"). Neither Tam nor his author was a solemn moralist: such morality as the poem has is not in the tongue-in-the-cheek warnings and reproaches, but in the spirit of human irrepressibility, that, even face to face with the Devil, cannot resist applauding the caperings of a buxom girl: "Weel done, cutty-sark!"

The text follows the first edition, apart from the addition of a semi-colon in l. 24.

> When chapmen billies leave the street,
> And drouthy neebors, neebors meet,
> As market-days are wearing late,
> And folk begin to tak the gate;
> 5 While we sit bowsing at the nappy,
> And gettin fou, and unco happy,
> We think na on the long Scots miles,
> The waters, mosses, slaps and styles,

1–8 *chapmen billies:* peddlar fellows.   *drouthy neebors:* thirsty neighbours.   *tak the gate:* go their ways.   *bowsing at the nappy:* swigging ale. *fou:* tight, drunk.   *unco:* very.   *long Scots miles:* A Scots mile was about 1,976 yards.   *mosses:* bogs.   *slaps:* gaps in fences and walls.

That lie between us and our hame,
10 Where sits out sulky, sullen dame,
Gathering her brows, like gathering storm,
Nursing her wrath to keep it warm.

This truth fand honest Tam o' Shanter,
As he frae Ayr ae night did canter;
15 (Auld Ayr, whom ne'er a town surpasses
For honest men and bonnie lasses.)

O Tam! hadst thou but been sae wise
As taen thy ain wife Kate's advice!
She tauld thee weel, thou was a skellum,
20 A bletherin, blusterin, drunken blellum;
That frae November till October,
Ae market-day thou was na sober;
That ilka melder, wi' the miller,
Thou sat as long as thou had siller;
25 That every naig was ca'd a shoe on,
The smith and thee gat roarin fou on;
That at the L—d's house, ev'n on Sunday,
Thou drank wi' Kirkton Jean till Monday.—
She prophesied that, late or soon,
30 Thou wad be found deep-drown'd in Doon;
Or catch'd wi' warlocks in the mirk
By Aloway's old haunted kirk.

13 *fand:* found.   *Tam o' Shanter:* The story is said to have been based on an adventure of a drunken farmer who lived at Shanter farm near Kirkoswald.

18–24 *As taen:* as to have taken.   *skellum:* ne'er-do-well.   *bletherin:* idly chattering.   *blellum:* babbler.   *Ae:* one.   *ilka melder:* every corn-grinding.   *siller:* money.

25 every nag that was shod.

28 *Kirkton Jean:* reputedly Jean Kennedy, a public-house keeper at Kirkoswald (or Kirkton). Most of the people and places in the poem have been identified.

30 *Doon:* the river in Ayrshire on which the town of Alloway stands.

31–32 *warlocks:* male witches.   *mirk:* darkness.   *kirk:* church.

Ah, gentle dames! it gars me greet,
To think how mony counsels sweet,
35 How mony lengthen'd sage advices,
The husband frae the wife despises!

But to our tale:—Ae market-night,
Tam had got planted unco right,
Fast by an ingle bleezing finely,
40 Wi' reamin swats that drank divinely;
And at his elbow, souter Johnie,
His ancient, trusty, drouthy cronie;
Tam lo'ed him like a vera brither,
They had been fou for weeks tegither.—
45 The night drave on wi' sangs and clatter,
And ay the ale was growing better:
The landlady and Tam grew gracious,
With favors secret, sweet, and precious:
The souter tauld his queerest stories;
50 The landlord's laugh was ready chorus:
The storm without might rair and rustle,
Tam did na mind the storm a whistle.—
Care, mad to see a man sae happy,
E'en drown'd himself amang the nappy:
55 As bees flee hame, wi' lades o' treasure,
The minutes wing'd their way wi' pleasure:
Kings may be blest, but Tam was glorious;
O'er a' the ills o' life victorious!

But pleasures are like poppies spread,
60 You seize the flower, its bloom is shed;
Or like the snow falls in the river,
A moment white—then melts for ever;

33–55 *gars me greet:* makes me weep.   *ingle:* fire.   *bleezing:* blazing.
reaming swats: foaming tankards of ale.   *souter:* cobbler.   *clatter:*
chatter.   *grew gracious:* became affectionate.   *rair:* roar.   *lades:*
loads.
61 *snow falls:* snow that falls.

Or like the borealis race,
That flit ere you can point their place;
65   Or like the rainbow's lovely form,
Evanishing amid the storm.—
Nae man can tether time or tide,
The hour approaches Tam maun ride;
That hour o' night's black arch the key-stane,
70   That dreary hour he mounts his beast in;
And sic a night he taks the road in
As ne'er poor sinner was abroad in.

The wind blew, as 'twad blawn its last;
The rattling showers rose on the blast;
75   The speedy gleams the darkness swallow'd
Loud, deep, and lang, the thunder bellow'd:
That night, a child might understand
The deil had business on his hand.

Weel mounted on his grey meare, Meg,
80   A better never lifted leg,
Tam skelpit on thro' dub and mire,
Despising wind, and rain, and fire:
Whyles holding fast his gude blue bonnet;
Whyles crooning o'er an auld Scots sonnet;
85   Whyles glowring round wi' prudent cares,
Lest bogles catch him unawares;
Kirk-Aloway was drawing nigh,
Where ghaists and houlets nightly cry.

By this time he was cross the ford,
90   Where in the snaw the chapman smoor'd;

63–78 *race:* kind, family.   *maun:* must.   *as 'twad:* as if it would
have.   *deil:* devil.

79–88 *meare:* mare.   *skelpit:* spanked along.   *dub:* puddle.   *fire:*
lightning.   *Whyles:* sometimes.   *sonnet:* song.   *glowring:* staring.
bogles: spooks, hobgoblins.   *ghaists:* ghosts.   *houlets:* owls.

90 *smoor'd:* was smothered.

And past the birks and meikle stane,
Where drunken Charlie brak's neck-bane;
And thro' the whins, and by the cairn,
Where hunters fand the murder'd bairn;
95 And near the tree, aboon the well,
Where Mungo's mither hang'd hersel:
Before him, Doon pours all his floods;
The doubling storm roars thro' the woods;
The light'nings flash from pole to pole;
100 Near, and more near, the thunders roll;
When, glimmering thro' groaning trees,
Kirk-Alloway seem'd in a bleeze;
Thro' ilka bore the beams were glancing,
And loud resounded mirth and dancing.

105   Inspiring, bold John Barleycorn!
What dangers thou canst make us scorn:
Wi' tippenny, we fear nae evil;
Wi' usquebae, we'll face the devil!
The swats sae ream'd in Tammie's noddle,
110 Fair-play, he car'd na deils a boddle:
But Maggie stood, right sair astonish'd,
Till by the heel and hand admonish'd,
She ventur'd forward on the light,
And, wow! Tam saw an unco sight!

115   Warlocks and witches in a dance,
Nae cotillon brent new frae France,

91–103 *birks:* birches.   *meikle stane:* great stone.   *brak's neck-bane:*
broke his neck.   *whins:* gorse.   *cairn:* heap of stones.   *aboon:* above.
bore: chink, hole.

105–8 *John Barleycorn:* personification of malt liquor.   *tippeny:* ale
sold at twopence a Scots pint (about three imperial pints).   *usquebae:*
whisky.

110 *Fair-play:* probably means "given fair play, or a fair chance", but
possibly means "to tell the truth, to give him his due".   *he car'd na deils
a boddle:* He didn't give a farthing for devils.

111–14 *sair:* sorely, extremely.   *unco:* extraordinary.

116 *cotillon:* cotillion, a French dance.   *brent new:* brand-new.

But hornpipes, jigs, strathspeys and reels,
Put life and mettle in their heels.—
A winnock-bunker in the East,
120 There sat auld Nick in shape o' beast;
A towzie tyke, black, grim, and large;
To gie them music was his charge:
He screw'd the pipes and gart them skirl,
Till roof and rafters a' did dirl.—
125 Coffins stood round, like open presses,
That shaw'd the dead in their last dresses;
And (by some deevilish cantraip slight)
Each in its cauld hand held a light;
By which heroic Tam was able
130 To note upon the haly table,
A murderer's banes, in gibbet-airns;
Twa span-lang, wee, unchirsten'd bairns;
A thief, new cutted frae a rape,
Wi' his last gasp his gab did gape;
135 Five tomahawks, wi' blood red-rusted;
Five scymitars, wi' murder crusted;
A garter which a babe had strangled;
A knife a father's throat had mangled,
Whom his ain son of life bereft,
140 The grey hairs yet stak to the heft:
Wi' mair of horrible and awefu',
That even to name wad be unlawfu':—
Three lawyers' tongues, turn'd inside out,
Wi' lies seam'd like a beggar's clout;
145 Three priests' hearts, rotten, black as muck,
Lay stinking, vile, in every neuk.

119–124 *A winnock-bunker:* in a window-aperture.   *towzie tyke:* scruffy
cur.   *screw'd:* squeezed.   *gart them skirl:* made them shriek.   *dirl:* rattle.
125–46 *presses:* tall cupboards.   *cantraip slight:* magic or supernatural
trick.   *the haly table:* the altar.   *gibbet-airns:* iron bands which fastened
bodies to the gallows.   *span-lang:* the length of a hand's span (about
nine inches).   *unchirsten'd bairns:* unchristened babies.   *rape:* rope.
gab: mouth.   *stak to the heft:* stuck to the handle.   *seam'd:* greasy.
clout: rag.   *neuk:* corner.

As Tammie glowr'd, amaz'd and curious,
The mirth and fun grew fast and furious:
The piper loud and louder blew;
150   The dancers quick and quicker flew;
They reel'd, they set, they cross'd, they cleekit,
Till ilka Carlin swat and reekit,
And coost her duddies on the wark,
And linket at it in her sark.—

155   Now Tam! O Tam! had thae been queans,
A' plump and strappin in their teens!
Their sarks, instead o' creeshie flainen,
Been snaw-white, seventeen-hunder linen;
Thir breeks o' mine, my only pair,
160   That ance were plush o' gude blue hair,
I wad hae gien·them off my hurdies
For ae blink o' the bonie burdies!
But withered beldams, auld and droll,
Rigwoodie hags wad spean a foal,
165   Loupin and flingin on a crumock,
I wonder did na turn thy stomach.—

But Tam kend what was what fu' brawlie;
There was ae winsome wench and walie,

151 This line refers to various steps in the dance. *Set* means "formed sets or groups", and *cleekit* means "linked together or joined hands".

152 *Carlin:* woman, usually one well past her prime.

153 cast off her ragged clothes to get down to the job of dancing.

154 tripped about in her shirt.

155-7 *queans:* wenches.   *creeshie flainen:* greasy flannel.

158 *seventeen-hunder linen:* a fine linen woven with a reed (i.e. an appliance for separating the warp threads) of seventeen hundred divisions.

159-65 *Thir breeks:* these breeches.   *plush:* a material with a deeper pile than velvet.   *gien:* given.   *hurdies:* haunches.   *blink:* glimpse. *burdies:* lasses.   *beldams:* old women.   *Rigwoodie:* bony and tough. *spean:* wean (i.e. even a foal would not feed from them).   *Loupin and flingin:* leaping and twirling.   *crumock:* a rough staff with a curved head used for support in walking.

167-8 *kend:* knew.   *fu' brawlie:* very well.   *walie:* buxom, comely.

That night enlisted in the core,
170   (Lang after kend on Carrick shore;
For mony a beast to dead she shot,
And perish'd mony a bonnie boat,
And shook baith meikle corn and bear
And kept the country-side in fear)—
175   Her cutty-sark o' Paisley harn,
That while a lassie she had worn,
In longitude tho' sorely scanty,
It was her best, and she was vauntie.—
Ah! little thought thy reverend graunie,
180   That sark she coft for her wee Nannie
Wi' twa pund Scots ('twas a' her riches)
Should ever grac'd a dance o' witches!

But here my Muse her wing maun cour,
Sic flights are far beyond her power;
185   To sing how Nannie lap and flang,
(A souple jad she was and strang,)
And how Tam stood like ane bewitch'd,
And thought his very een enrich'd;
Even Satan glowr'd, and fidg'd fu' fain,
190   And hotch'd, and blew wi' might and main;
Till first ae caper—syne anither—
Tam lost his reason a'thegither,
And roars out—"Weel done, cutty-sark!"
And in an instant all was dark;
195   And scarcely had he Maggie rallied,
When out the hellish legion sallied.—

169–72 *core:* company. *kend:* known. *Carrick:* a division of Ayrshire. *perish'd:* caused to perish.

173 damaged large quantities of oats and barley.

175 her short shirt of coarse Paisley linen.

178–82 *vauntie:* proud of it. *graunie:* granny. *coft:* bought. *twa punds Scots:* A "pund Scots" was worth about twenty pence. *ever grac'd:* ever have graced.

183–91 *maun cour:* must fold timidly. *sic:* such. *lap and flang:* See l. 165. *souple jad:* supple wench. *een:* eyes. *fidg'd fu' fain:* wriggled with delight. *hotch'd:* jerked about. *syne:* then afterwards.

As bees bizz out wi' angry fyke,
When plundering herds assail their byke;
As open pussie's mortal foes,
200 When, pop, she starts before their nose;
As eager rins the market-croud,
When "catch the thief!" resounds aloud;
So Maggy rins, the witches follow,
Wi' mony an eldritch shout and hollo.—

205 Ah Tam! ah Tam! thou'll get thy fairin!
In hell they'll roast thee like a herrin!
In vain thy Kate awaits thy comin,
Kate soon will be a woefu' woman!!!
Now, do thy speedy utmost, Meg!
210 And win the key-stane o' the brig;
There at them thou thy tail may toss,
A running stream they dare na cross!
But ere the key-stane she could make,
The fient a tail she had to shake;
215 For Nannie, far before the rest,
Hard upon noble Maggy prest,
And flew at Tam wi' furious ettle,
But little kend she Maggy's mettle!
Ae spring brought off her master hale,
220 But left behind her ain gray tail:
The carlin claught her by the rump,
And left poor Maggy scarce a stump.

Now wha this Tale o' truth shall read,
Ilk man and mother's son, take heed:

197–204 *fyke:* bustle.   *herds:* herdsmen and shepherds.   *byke:* nest.
open: give tongue (a hunting expression).   *pussie's:* the hare's (her mortal
foes are the hounds).   *eldritch:* uncanny.

205 *fairin:* reward.   210 *win:* gain, reach.

212 In a letter to George Grose, Burns mentioned that "no diabolical
power can pursue you beyond the middle of a running stream".

214–21 *The fient a tail:* the devil a tail (i.e. no tail).   *ettle:* intention.
hale: whole, safe and sound.   *claught:* clutched.

223–4 *wha:* whoever.   *Ilk:* every.

225   Whene'er to drink you are inclin'd,
       Or cutty-sarks rin in your mind,
       Think, ye may buy the joys o'er dear;
       Remember TAM O' SHANTER'S MEARE!

227 *o'er dear:* too dearly.

Samuel Taylor Coleridge

FROST AT MIDNIGHT

THE quarto pamphlet, *Fears in Solitude, written in 1798, during the alarm of an invasion. To which are added, Famine, An Ode; and Frost at Midnight,* which Coleridge published in 1798, included a prospect poem relating to a political situation ("Fears in Solitude") as well as a nocturnal. Cowper, too, had watched on a frosty night the sooty films fluttering on the grate, and had connected them with an "indolent vacuity of thought" and with the activity of an imagination creating what it saw (see page 165); but, whereas he briefly dismissed the superstition attached to such films, Coleridge allowed it to lead him back to memories of a lonely childhood, and, by contrast, to the natural education he planned for his infant son, Hartley, asleep at his side. The poem, with its hesitations and sudden leaps, recreates the mood of reverie, and yet beneath its apparently casual and wandering manner, there is a process of thought and imagination culminating in the magnificent recall of the frosty night.

In later versions Coleridge condensed lines 19–29, made some local improvements (particularly the substitution of *frost* for *cold* in line 77), and cut away the last six lines. The way in which the excision of these lines turned a very good poem into a great one is so fine an illustration of a neglected aspect of the art of poetry, that the only justification for printing the poem in its original form is that it shows how an act of self-criticism can be an act of creation.

> The Frost performs its secret ministry,
> Unhelp'd by any wind. The owlet's cry
> Came loud—and hark, again! loud as before.
> The inmates of my cottage, all at rest,

4 *my cottage:* The poem was written in Coleridge's cottage at Nether Stowey, Somerset.

5   Have left me to that solitude, which suits
    Abstruser musings: save that at my side
    My cradled infant slumbers peacefully.
    'Tis calm indeed! so calm, that it disturbs
    And vexes meditation with its strange
10 And extreme silentness. Sea, hill, and wood,
    This populous village! Sea, and hill, and wood,
    With all the numberless goings on of life,
    Inaudible as dreams! the thin blue flame
    Lies on my low-burnt fire, and quivers not:
15 Only that film, which flutter'd on the grate,
    Still flutters there, the sole unquiet thing,
    Methinks, its motion in this hush of nature
    Gives it dim sympathies with me, who live,
    Making it a companionable form,
20 With which I can hold commune. Idle thought!
    But still the living spirit in our frame,
    That loves not to behold a lifeless thing,
    Transfuses into all its own delights
    Its own volition, sometimes with deep faith,
25 And sometimes with fantastic playfulness.
    Ah me! amus'd by no such curious toys
    Of the self-watching subtilizing mind,
    How often in my early school-boy days,
    With most believing superstitious wish
30 Presageful have I gaz'd upon the bars,
    To watch the *stranger* there! and oft belike,
    With unclos'd lids, already had I dreamt
    Of my sweet birthplace, and the old church-tower,
    Whose bells, the poor man's only music, rang
35 From morn to evening, all the hot fair-day,

7 *My cradled infant:* Hartley Coleridge, born 1796.

15 *film:* "Only that *film*. In all parts of the kingdom, these films are
called *strangers*, and supposed to portend the arrival of some absent friend."
(*Coleridge, 1798*). Cf. *The Task*, p. 165, ll. 49 ff. Humphry House compares
the two passages in *Coleridge: The Clark Lectures, 1951–2* (Hart-Davis, 1953).

33 *birthplace:* Coleridge was born at The Vicarage in Ottery St. Mary,
Devonshire, famous for its beautiful church.

So sweetly, that they stirr'd and haunted me
With a wild pleasure, falling on mine ear
Most like articulate sounds of things to come!
So gaz'd I, till the soothing things, I dreamt,
40 Lull'd me to sleep, and sleep prolong'd my dreams!
And so I brooded all the following morn,
Aw'd by the stern preceptor's face, mine eye
Fix'd with mock study on my swimming book:
Save if the door half-open'd, and I snatch'd
45 A hasty glance, and still my heart leapt up,
For still I hop'd to see the *stranger's* face,
Townsman, or aunt, or sister more belov'd,
My play-mate when we both were cloth'd alike!

Dear babe, that sleepest cradled by my side,
50 Whose gentle breathings, heard in this dead calm,
Fill up the interspersed vacancies
And momentary pauses of the thought!
My babe so beautiful! it fills my heart
With tender gladness, thus to look at thee,
55 And think, that thou shalt learn far other lore,
And in far other scenes! For I was rear'd
In the great city, pent mid cloisters dim,
And saw nought lovely but the sky and stars.
But *thou*, my babe! Shalt wander, like a breeze,
60 By lakes and sandy shores, beneath the crags
Of ancient mountain, and beneath the clouds,
Which image in their bulk both lakes and shores
And mountain crags: so shalt thou see and hear
The lovely shapes and sounds intelligible
65 Of that eternal language, which thy God
Utters, who from eternity doth teach
Himself in all, and all things in himself.
Great universal Teacher! he shall mould
Thy spirit, and by giving make it ask.

57 *the great city:* Coleridge's school was Christ's Hospital, then situated
in the City of London.

70 Therefore all seasons shall be sweet to thee,
Whether the summer clothe the general earth
With greenness, or the redbreasts sit and sing
Betwixt the tufts of snow on the bare branch
Of mossy apple-tree, while all the thatch
75 Smokes in the sun-thaw: whether the eave-drops fall
Heard only in the trances of the blast,
Or whether the secret ministery of cold
Shall hang them up in silent icicles,
Quietly shining to the quiet moon,
80 Like those, my babe! which, ere to-morrow's warmth
Have capp'd their sharp keen points with pendulous drops,
Will catch thine eye, and with their novelty
Suspend thy little soul; then make thee shout,
And stretch and flutter from thy mother's arms
85 As thou would'st fly for very eagerness.

February 1798.

William Wordsworth

LINES WRITTEN A FEW MILES ABOVE TINTERN ABBEY, ON REVISITING THE BANKS OF THE WYE DURING A TOUR, JULY, 13, 1798

ALTHOUGH Wordsworth did not call his poem an ode, he hoped "that in the transitions and the impassioned music of the versification, would be found the principal requisites of that species of composition". The reference to "transitions" is a reminder that, for all the unstrained natural eloquence of the poem and the suggestion of impromptu in the particularity of the title, "Tintern Abbey" is as carefully constructed as Gray's *Elegy*, with its three main divisions following the introductory prospect—the threefold benefits the poet had derived from the scene, the three stages in his relationship to it, the peroration to his sister—and the whole beautifully rounded off in the last few lines by discreet echoes of words and phrases from the beginning. Though for Wordsworth poetry was "the spontaneous overflow of powerful feelings", it was also Wordsworth who declared "Again and again I must repeat, that the composition of verse is infinitely more of

an art than men are prepared to believe; and absolute success in it depends
upon innumerable minutiae." (To William Rowan Hamilton, November
22, 1831.)
The text is that of the first edition of *Lyrical Ballads and Poems* (1798).

> Five years have passed; five summers, with the length
> Of five long winters! and again I hear
> These waters, rolling from their mountain-springs
> With a sweet inland murmur.—Once again
> 5 Do I behold these steep and lofty cliffs,
> Which on a wild secluded scene impress
> Thoughts of more deep seclusion; and connect
> The landscape with the quiet of the sky.
> The day is come when I again repose
> 10 Here, under this dark sycamore, and view
> These plots of cottage-ground, these orchard-tufts,
> Which, at this season, with their unripe fruits,
> Among the woods and copses lose themselves,
> Nor, with their green and simple hue, disturb
> 15 The wild green landscape. Once again I see
> These hedge-rows, hardly hedge-rows, little lines
> Of sportive wood run wild; these pastoral farms
> Green to the very door; and wreathes of smoke
> Sent up, in silence, from among the trees,
> 20 And the low copses—coming from the trees
> With some uncertain notice, as might seem,
> Of vagrant dwellers in the houseless woods,
> Or of some hermit's cave, where by his fire

4 *inland murmur:* "The river is not affected by the tides a few miles above
Tintern." (*Wordsworth, 1798.*)

11 *orchard-tufts:* Cf. *Windsor-Forest*, p. 43, l. 27 n.

17 *pastoral:* strictly refers to sheep-farms—but, here probably means with
pasture-land.

20 According to the "Errata" page of *Lyrical Ballads* (1798) this line should
be omitted, presumably because it is pointlessly repetitive.

23 *hermit's cave:* One wonders how many hermits were inhabiting caves
in the Wye valley in 1798. Perhaps this is an example of Wordsworth's
imagination being coloured by the numerous hermits and recluses of
eighteenth-century poetry.

The hermit sits alone.

                                      Though absent long,
25   These forms of beauty have not been to me,
     As is a landscape to a blind man's eye:
     But oft, in lonely rooms, and mid the din
     Of towns and cities, I have owed to them,
     In hours of weariness, sensations sweet,
30   Felt in the blood, and felt along the heart,
     And passing even into my purer mind
     With tranquil restoration:—feelings too
     Of unremembered pleasure; such, perhaps,
     As may have had no trivial influence
35   On that best portion of a good man's life;
     His little, nameless, unremembered acts
     Of kindness and of love. Nor less, I trust,
     To them I may have owed another gift,
     Of aspect more sublime; that blessed mood,
40   In which the burthen of the mystery,
     In which the heavy and the weary weight
     Of all this unintelligible world
     Is lighten'd:—that serene and blessed mood,
     In which the affections gently lead us on,
45   Until, the breath of this corporeal frame,
     And even the motion of our human blood
     Almost suspended, we are laid asleep
     In body, and become a living soul:
     While with an eye made quiet by the power
50   Of harmony, and the deep power of joy,
     We see into the life of things.

                                         If this
     Be but a vain belief, yet, oh! how oft,
     In darkness, and amid the many shapes
     Of joyless day-light; when the fretful stir
55   Unprofitable, and the fever of the world,
     Have hung upon the beatings of my heart,
     How oft, in spirit, have I turned to thee

O sylvan Wye! Thou wanderer through the wood
How often has my spirit turned to thee!
60   And now, with gleams of half-extinguish'd thought,
With many recognitions dim and faint,
And somewhat of a sad perplexity,
The picture of the mind revives again:
While here I stand, not only with the sense
65   Of present pleasure, but with pleasing thoughts
That in this moment there is life and food
For future years. And so I dare to hope
Though changed, no doubt, from what I was, when first
I came among these hills; when like a roe
70   I bounded o'er the mountains, by the sides
Of the deep rivers, and the lonely streams,
Wherever nature led; more like a man
Flying from something that he dreads, than one
Who sought the thing he loved. For nature then
75   (The coarser pleasures of my boyish days,
And their glad animal movements all gone by,)
To me was all in all.—I cannot paint
What then I was. The sounding cataract
Haunted me like a passion: the tall rock,
80   The mountain, and the deep and gloomy wood,
Their colours and their forms, were then to me
An appetite: a feeling and a love,
That had no need of a remoter charm,
By thought supplied, or any interest
85   Unborrowed from the eye.—That time is past,
And all its aching joys are now no more,
And all its dizzy raptures. Not for this
Faint I, nor mourn nor murmur: other gifts
Have followed, for such loss, I would believe,
90   Abundant recompence. For I have learned
To look on nature, not as in the hour
Of thoughtless youth, but hearing oftentimes
The still, sad music of humanity,

58 *sylvan:* wooded.
63 The mental image of the Wye is revived.

Not harsh nor grating, though of ample power
95 To chasten and subdue. And I have felt
A presence that disturbs me with the joy
Of elevated thoughts; a sense sublime
Of something far more deeply interfused,
Whose dwelling is the light of setting suns,
100 And the round ocean, and the living air,
And the blue sky, and in the mind of man,
A motion and a spirit, that impels
All thinking things, all objects of all thought,
And rolls through all things. Therefore am I still
105 A lover of the meadows and the woods,
And mountains; and of all that we behold
From this green earth; of all the mighty world
Of eye and ear, both what they half-create,
And what perceive; well pleased to recognize
110 In nature and the language of the sense,
The anchor of my purest thoughts, the nurse,
The guide, the guardian of my heart, and soul
Of all my moral being.

Nor, perchance,
If I were not thus taught, should I the more
115 Suffer my genial spirits to decay:
For thou art with me, here, upon the banks
. Of this fair river; thou, my dearest Friend,

---

108 *half-create:* "This line has a close resemblance to an admirable line
of Young, the exact expression of which I cannot recollect." (*Wordsworth,
1798.*) Wordsworth probably had in mind a passage in "Night VI" of
Night-Thoughts where Young says that men "half create the wondrous
World they see". Young's case is that but for man's senses "Earth were a
rude, uncolour'd Chaos still". It is human senses which create taste, harmony,
radiance and so on.

115 *genial:* healthful.

117 *my dearest Friend:* Dorothy Wordsworth, who accompanied her
brother on this tour. In her, Wordsworth found not only a faithful and
loving disciple, but also a companion who (as her *Journals* show) had a
sensitivity and poetic gift of her own.

My dear, dear Friend, and in thy voice I catch
The language of my former heart, and read
120   My former pleasures in the shooting lights
Of thy wild eyes. Oh! yet a little while
May I behold in thee what I was once,
My dear, dear Sister! And this prayer I make,
Knowing that Nature never did betray
125   The heart that loved her; 'tis her privilege,
Through all the years of this our life, to lead
From joy to joy: for she can so inform
The mind that is within us, so impress
With quietness and beauty, and so feed
130   With lofty thoughts, that neither evil tongues,
Rash judgments, nor the sneers of selfish men,
Nor greetings where no kindness is, nor all
The dreary intercourse of daily life,
Shall e'er prevail against us, or disturb
135   Our chearful faith that all which we behold
Is full of blessings. Therefore let the moon
Shine on thee in thy solitary walk;
And let the misty mountain winds be free
To blow against thee: and in after years,
140   When these wild ecstasies shall be matured
Into a sober pleasure, when thy mind
Shall be a mansion for all lovely forms,
Thy memory be as a dwelling-place
For all sweet sounds and harmonies; Oh! then,
145   If solitude, or fear, or pain, or grief,
Should be thy portion, with what healing thoughts
Of tender joy wilt thou remember me,
And these my exhortations! Nor, perchance,
If I should be, where I no more can hear
150   Thy voice, nor catch from thy wild eyes these gleams
Of past existence, wilt thou then forget
That on the banks of this delightful stream
We stood together; and that I, so long
A worshipper of Nature, hither came,
155   Unwearied in that service: rather say

With warmer love, oh! with far deeper zeal
Of holier love. Nor wilt thou then forget,
That after many wanderings, many years
Of absence, these steep woods and lofty cliffs,
160   And this green pastoral landscape, were to me
More dear, both for themselves, and for thy sake.